Spokesongs

Spokesongs

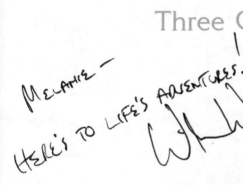

Bicycle Adventures on
Three Continents

MELANIE —
HERE'S TO LIFE'S ADVENTURES.

Willie Weir

BREAKAWAY BOOKS
HALCOTTSVILLE, NY
2000

Spokesongs: Bicycle Adventures on Three Continents

Copyright © 1997, 2000 Willie Weir

Excerpt from *Spokesong,* a play by Stewart Parker and Jimmy Kennedy. Copyright © 1984.

Second Edition

Printed in the United States of America

10 9 8 7 6 5 4 3 2 1

Library of Congress Catalog Card Number: 99-85884
ISBN: 1-891369-17-2

All photographs © Willie Weir unless noted

Book design, map illustrations by Kat Marriner

Published by Breakaway Books
P. O. Box 24
Halcottsville, NY 12438
(800) 548-4348
www.breakawaybooks.com

Distributed by Consortium

Visit **www.willieweir.com**

To my brother, Jeff,
for whom I began to write.

Contents

South Africa

The Balkans

I can hear the soft hum of the spokes
When I'm pedaling down a green hill
It's the song I first learned from my folks
and the melody follows me still

Song of the spokes, spokesong
Whisp'ring through the years
Music that's good for the ears

From *Spokesong*, a play
by Stewart Parker & Jimmy Kennedy

I can't remember precisely when my love affair with bicycle travel began: Perhaps it was while riding my three-speed Schwinn down to Thrifty drugstore to purchase fifteen-cent, triple-scoop ice cream cones that melted down my arm before I got halfway across the parking lot; or while riding my yellow, ten-speed Vista Esquire to the bowling alley with my fourteen-pound, name-engraved bowling ball perched on the top tube; or perhaps years later as a courier in Seattle, dodging city traffic, little old ladies, and attorneys on my Raleigh mountain bike. But when push comes to shove, I'd have to pin it down to a journey across the United States with my childhood buddy, Thomas. We didn't really know what we were doing—little planning, less money, and no training. We simply pedaled off from Seaside, Oregon, in July on our Univega Gran Turismo touring bikes and two months later found ourselves cycling down Second Avenue in New York City.

That trip was nineteen years, dozens of countries, and some forty thousand miles ago.

While on the road I have always kept my journals in the form of letters home to my brother, Jeff—my devoted audience of one. In 1994 my audience dramatically expanded with the opportunity to write for public radio station KUOW in Seattle. This book contains the stories (some expanded, some exactly as they aired) from three separate journeys: India, South Africa, and the Balkans.

They by no means begin to encompass the enormity and diversity of the experiences I had; that would take several volumes. I hope you enjoy them for what they are—verbal songs of the road. If these "spokesongs" make you smile or laugh or wonder, or inspire you to explore the world outside the organized tour packages and resorts of the world—my time has been well spent.

India

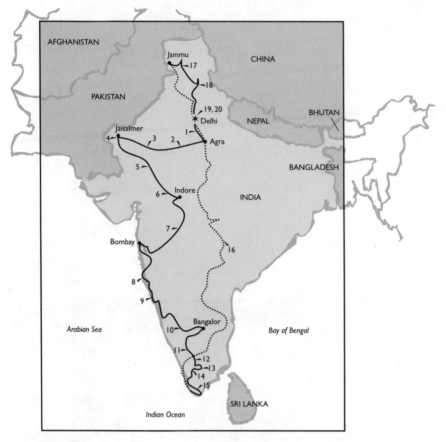

Bicycle Route ——
Train Route ········

December 1993–May 1994

Map Key

1 Road Warrior
2 Bicycle Circus
3 Charlie Brown Plays Cricket
4 The Bible
5 The Camel Club
6 A Night in Jail
7 The Bhagvati Binge
8 I Am God
9 Back Roads and Back Waters
10 Beached in Goa
11 Oh! Canada
12 Ear Cleaners
13 Climb Every Mountain
14 The Five Questions
15 Arnold
16 The Magic Word
17 Bent into Shape
18 The Himsagar Express
19 A Shepherd's Life for Me
20 Jalori Pass
21 Conned
22 Back to Delhi

In 1993, on the last day of a four-month bicycle tour in New Zealand, I met another cyclist, a Frenchman, and we swapped travel stories. He had recently traveled with his girlfriend through India. He couldn't stop talking about this strange, maddening, wonderful country. "You have to go there," he insisted. "I will," I said, as much to be polite as to keep him from hounding me about it. But I had no intention of following up on my shallow promise. Noise, pollution, crowded streets lined with beggars, disease … not my idea of a good time.

That same evening I cycled into Auckland. I had a place to stay with friends I had made while hiking on the South Island. Wendy greeted me at the door with a letter in her hand. It was from Richard and Jill, friends who were on a global bicycle journey on their tandem mountain bike. The letter had arrived in Seattle, been forwarded to my parents in California, and then forwarded to Wendy's address in New Zealand. It had journeyed around the world as well, having been mailed from … India.

After spending a grand evening with Wendy and her friends, I sat propped up against the headboard in her guest room, wishing for something to read. I searched the room and found one book. It was *City of Joy*, the story of a priest who lived in a slum of Calcutta, India.

That was three. Were these signs? Or just coincidences?

I soon forgot the day's events and busied myself with packing for my flight home.

One of the reasons I love traveling for any great length of time is that upon your return a mountain of mail awaits you. Yes, the bulk of it is bills and junk mail, but the sheer mass makes me feel important. I was busy sorting, dividing it into "personal" and "I'll get to it sooner or later," when I came upon an announcement from the airline I had all my frequent flier miles with. I opened it up and sat in openmouthed silence. The letter proudly announced one new destination ... New Delhi.

"What is it?" my brother asked.

"I'm going to India," I stammered.

"Why?"

"I have absolutely no idea."

Road Warrior

I ATTACKED HIGHWAY 2 SOUTH OUT OF DELHI. I FELT AS IF ALL 8.4 million residents of that city were on the same road: buses, cars, motor scooters, bicycles, pedestrians, carts pulled by oxen, horses, camels, even an elephant—all dodging and swerving in a vast sea of noise.

I made my own small contribution to the din, ringing my sturdy two-pound, Indian-made bicycle bell. In the subcontinent, if you are not making noise, you do not exist. I remember the phrase drummed into my head in primary school—"Stop, look, and listen." In India, it is "stop, listen, go." Within the first fifteen minutes of pedaling I had nearly run over three elderly woman, five students, and two dogs. In each instance, I had stopped ringing my bell to rest my throbbing thumb, thus rendering myself invisible.

The same goes for truckers. The philosophy appears to be "I Honk—Therefore I Am." Every truck has a sign on the back door or bumper that beseeches, "Horn Please." This is due to the fact that India is a country of 900 million people and fourteen rearview mirrors.

There are no vehicle emission standards in India. I'm quite sure I ingested my yearly allowance of diesel exhaust in one afternoon. Huge black clouds billowed out of every tailpipe. I rode bandit-style with a bandanna covering my nose and mouth. My skin glistened with a mixture of sweat and oil, and my throat ached.

My trip might have never begun, except for an elderly man, dressed all in white, carrying a large package covered with sewn burlap and sealing wax. I needed to cross the street in the center of New Delhi to merge onto the road to Agra. But there was no traffic light. I waited with my gear-laden Raleigh mountain bike for a break in the traffic. Fifteen minutes passed and I hadn't budged an inch. I was too fascinated by the mass of humanity and vehicles to be frustrated yet, but I needed to make a move. But every time I began to pull away from the curb, the rational part of my brain warned me that I was about to die.

Then the man with the package walked up next to me. I could see that he was going to cross the street. He had a look of calm and relaxation for someone who was about to tempt fate.

He moved in front of me. I tensed and focused on his back, trying to block out the tons of steel and flesh moving through my periphery. No matter what that small voice says, I promised, when he goes, I'll follow.

Then he simply began to walk. No panic. No darting or dodging. I followed so closely I thought I would clip his heels. I was Peter walking on water, and if I took my eyes off my package-bearing savior, I was going to sink in a sea of humanity.

I didn't look up until the white shirt in front of me paused. We were on the opposite side of the street. My journey could now safely begin. But before I could thank him, he quickly disappeared in a crowd of vegetable and grain sellers.

Merging in between a bicycle-taxi and a truck crammed with turkeys, I joined the outgoing flow of the masses leaving Delhi. After hours of battle with the relentless traffic, I began to relax enough to ease up on the death grip I had on my handlebars. I looked back and marveled at a family of four all perched on a motor scooter. I waved at the youngest girl. The girl's father smiled and nodded. Then his eyes suddenly widened. I lurched around just in time to see a man whipping an ox, pulling a cart full of enormous ceramic tiles bearing down on us going the wrong way.

I instantly learned the most important rule of the road: The bigger vehicle always has the right-of-way. This puts bicycles at the very bottom of the vehicle caste system. I quickly veered into the ditch and was quickly joined by my friends on the motor scooter and two pedestrians. In most parts of the world, this is getting run off the road. In India, it is yielding the right-of-way.

I managed to stay upright and merged back onto the highway. I passed a sign that read, "Calamity overtakes the man who rashly overtakes."

So I've survived my first encounter with India—crossing the street. I've been told by many a traveler to expect to come home from this spiritual country a wiser person. As I relax in the serene grounds of the Taj Mahal, the only words of wisdom I can impart: Carpool everyone. Carpool.

Bicycle Circus

THERE SEEMS TO BE ONLY ONE STYLE AND MAKE OF BICYCLE IN INDIA—a black single-speed with upright handlebars and fenders. It apparently comes in only one size as well, as I have seen countless Indian boys riding bikes so large that one slip could dash all hopes of ever enjoying sexual intercourse.

The problem this homogeneity poses is that riding a multi-colored, twenty-one-speed mountain bike with bar-ends and panniers is the equivalent of the circus coming to town.

Whenever I pass another cyclist there is the inevitable "squeak, squeak, rattle, rattle, clunk" as he speeds up to pass. (I use "he" because I can count on one hand the number of girls I've seen riding bicycles so far.) Once he has successfully passed, wearing a determined grin, he stops pedaling and turns around to get a better look—forcing a radical swerve to avoid collision. This frustrating leapfrog can go on for kilometers.

Riding through or stopping in a town multiplies the problem. Just yesterday I stopped at a market and ordered some chai (tea boiled with milk, cardamom, and as much sugar as will hold in solution). First there were five boys and three men observing my mechanical wonder. Their numbers soon increased to twenty. Then sixty. Within three minutes, 150 bodies surrounded me, closing in like a human vise, inching in for a better view or a touch.

A rather helpless feeling creeps over you when that many people collectively invade your personal space. I took a slow, deep breath and fought my urge to scream.

India is an assault on your senses. A place where you redefine *extreme*. In one week I had already determined India to be the loudest, most peaceful, smelliest, most colorful, most horrific, most crowded, ugliest, most beautiful place I had ever encountered.

I spent my first five days as a walking, cycling exposed nerve. My shoulders appeared to be permanently attached to my earlobes. "India would be a wonderful place to travel," I thought, "if only people wouldn't stare. If only they'd stop crowding me. If only everyone didn't want to sell me something. If only they'd all shut up."

I had planned to travel the subcontinent for five months. I wasn't going to last a week.

Then a man in a village market who was selling clay pots out of a small metal cart gave me all the advice I needed in one softly spoken sentence.

I had cycled into a town and one by one picked up over sixty boys who, enthralled with my bike, chased me down the street. Having already been through this dozens of times, I knew I wasn't going to lose them, so I stopped at the man's cart and hoped they would finally get bored and go away.

All the boys slowly edged in as close to my bicycle as they possibly could. One hundred and twenty feet shuffled. One hundred and twenty eyes stared.

The man saw my frustration. He put his hand up to his enormous mustache, leaned over, and said, "It is better to change your own mind than to try and change the minds of 900 million others."

I glanced down at the juvenile mob. One small boy gently petted my bike. Just maybe, if he stroked it long enough, it would follow him home. I was straddling a most magical machine: a bicycle of such magnificence that he could only dream of owning one like it. Wouldn't I chase it down the street if I was eight years old?

I glanced up at the merchant. His intense yet gentle eyes spoke volumes. The tension melted. My shoulders relaxed. I stopped fighting India and instead, sighed into it.

I pedaled through the rest of the town, picking up more boys along the way. But I pedaled slowly, waving to the new kids who joined the cluster.

Nothing had changed about the situation. I was still being tailed by a mob of overly eager kids who would not go away until I had pedaled far beyond their town. But for the first time since I had arrived in India, I was smiling.

Charlie Brown Plays Cricket

I WAS THE CHARLIE BROWN OF MY LITTLE LEAGUE BASEBALL TEAM. The only time I got on base was when walked or hit by a pitch. I remember other teammates' fathers yelling, "Lean in, Willie. Lean in." I was so afraid of the ball that I once feigned a migraine headache to avoid coming up to the plate against an older kid who towered over everyone and threw a wicked fastball (at least twenty-five miles an hour).

My batting average stood rock solid at .000, and before the last game of the season my manager offered me ten dollars if I got a hit. The season ended—my manager's net worth remained the same.

That sums up my entire baseball career. One disastrous season. Soon thereafter I took up bowling, a sport in which you get to hurl a heavy ball without the fear of ever having someone hurl it back at you.

But I went on to be an avid baseball fan. Maybe it is my absolute awe and admiration for anybody who can stand up to a ninety-mile-an-hour fastball without closing his eyes. I spent the summer of my thirteenth year with a transistor radio glued to my ear listening to the 1974 Oakland A's. Reggie Jackson. Sal Bando. Campy Campanarus. Joe Rudy. I knew them all.

When I moved to Seattle in 1985, I immediately became a Mariners fan. This took some getting used to. Not only were the Mariners at the time one of the worst teams in baseball, but they had the disadvantage of playing inside a massive concrete dome. But I still faithfully showed up at the park. I sat in the Kingdome for so many hours with my Mariners hopelessly behind that, to alleviate boredom, I learned how to sing both "Take Me Out to the Ballgame" and "The Star-Spangled Banner" … backward.

But in 1989 the Mariners brought up Ken Griffey Jr. From then on it didn't matter if the M's lost by ten runs; Griffey made it worth going to the park. At some point during a nine-inning game, whether it was a colossal home run, a humanly impossible diving catch, or a laser-beam throw to second base, Griffey made it worth sitting for four-plus hours in artificial light on hard metal bleachers.

In India, baseball does not exist, but its historical predecessor, cricket, reigns supreme. Boys of all ages can be seen playing in schoolyards, fields, street corners, and back alleys. It is not uncommon to come across a crowd of sixty men, all gathered outside the window of a shop, staring in at a small black-and-white TV, transfixed by the men in white. When India lost a match to Pakistan I observed the entire country go into collective depression.

In the late afternoon, as I pedaled through a small village in Rajasthan, I noticed a large group of boys practicing their national sport. They waved me over and one boy yelled, "Do you play?" Before I had a chance to reply, I had a fat cricket bat in my hands and stood in front of the wickets. The tallest boy said, "I throw slow," and prepared with a short run to pitch or "bowl" the ball.

Having observed others playing, I knew to position the bat down by my feet as if I were preparing to hit a golf ball, but the laughter around me confirmed my stance was still unconventional.

The boy tossed the ball and it bounced right. I swung and missed. Over twenty years had passed and my fortune hadn't changed. The boy announced, "Fast now," and smiled. Hadn't I borne enough humiliation? I slammed down the bat and headed for my bike. But a Little Leaguer's voice whispered, "C'mon Willie. Don't think Charlie Brown. Think Ken Griffey Jr."

I picked up the bat and dug in. The boy took the longest run legally allowed and hurled the ball with all his thirteen-year-old might. The ball bounced and I swung wildly, connecting with a loud "thwack." The ball sailed over the head of the pitcher, over the heads of the boys out in the field, and disappeared behind some large boulders.

Suddenly I was surrounded by cheering boys, jumping up and down and patting me on the back, several of whom were shouting, "Six! Six!"

I had just enough knowledge of cricket to know what that meant. It had taken thirty-two years and a journey halfway around the world— but I had hit a home run.

The Bible

THE LONELY PLANET TRAVEL SURVIVAL KIT IS BY FAR THE MOST popular series of travel guidebooks in the world. The India edition is so widely used it is known by travelers as "the Bible."

I was carrying one, all 1,099 pages of it. You would have never known, though. It stayed buried deep in my panniers, only to be referenced when I was behind closed doors. You see, it's hard to keep up the adventure-cyclist image while standing on a street corner with your nose buried in a guidebook.

While cycling through the desert, west from Jaipur, I had plenty of time to peruse the information about accommodations in the fort city of Jaisalmer. With the three top-quality cheap hotels committed to memory, I cycled into the city limits with my guidebook far from sight, buried deeply in my left rear pannier.

Seven hundred miles into my trip, I climbed the road that edged along the walls of the ancient fort and into the city center. As I crested the hill, a man jumped out into the middle of the street, blocking any further progress.

"Where are you going?"

I quickly sensed this guy was one of those pushy touts who was going to try to sell me on an expensive hotel.

"I'm heading for a place to stay, but I don't need any help, thank you."

I started to lean forward, ready to run him over, if necessary.

"What does your Bible say?"

All momentum stopped.

"My Bible? What are you talking about?"

"It is the blue book. Every one of you has one. Don't try and deny it. Somewhere on this bicycle there is a Bible."

I was so caught off guard, my lying reflex was jammed. "You're right," I said. "It is in that one there." I pointed at the pannier.

He smiled with an "I knew it" flair and then leaned in close and asked, "How do you get into this Bible of yours? I have a small hotel here and I am going broke because I am not in the Bible." He didn't wait for my response. "Where are you staying tonight?"

"The Fort Jaisalmer Hotel," I answered.

"Fine. Go." He waved his hands. "Go. Go. I will wait for you right here." Then he folded his arms and wiggled his head and smiled, "You will be back."

I pedaled on, thinking, "Yeah, right, buddy."

Ten minutes later I walked into the Fort Jaisalmer Hotel … and it was an absolute dump. The rooms were filthy and twice as expensive as my newly updated guidebook quoted. The management had obviously realized that because their establishment had landed in the Lonely Planet, they could fire the cleaning staff and jack up the rates … and the travelers would still flock there. Like lemmings they'd disembark from buses and trains, every one of them warned not to be led astray by the touts and thieves on every corner.

It dawned on me that every time I opened and followed my guidebook, I was taking someone else's adventure, not my own. The writer had taken his or her adventure months, if not years, prior to my purchasing the hollowed scriptures. I walked out of the hotel.

It must have been at least forty-five minutes, but there he was, just as he promised.

"I told you. I told you, you would be back."

He introduced himself as Prakash and led me to his family's hotel. My room was spotlessly clean, with marble floors and a private bath, and half the price of the smallest room at the other hotel. Prakash took me on a tour of the city. Jaisalmer is unique in that most of the city's population still lives within the walls of the fort. The shaded, narrow streets were a welcome respite from the desert sun.

We wound through the maze, dodging children and goats. In the course of the afternoon we stopped in for visits with three of his brothers, his barber (who gave me a quick trim and a shave), and his childhood friend who works for the police, always stopping long enough for a cup of chai.

The next morning I ate breakfast not with German and Swiss tourists, but with Prakash and his entire family.

Now, I'm not saying guidebooks are inherently evil, but the experience led me to rewrite the lyrics to a Bible-camp song from my youth. I sing it when I'm tempted to follow someone else's path.

Thirty rupees, this I know,
For the Bible tells me so.
Single room with bath and fan
And a beach where I can tan.

Chorus:
The Planet guides me.
Lonely Planet guides me.
The Planet guides me.
It's all I need to know.

Came to India to stay,
From my budget I can't stray.
Don't like to talk to locals much,
LPG's my favorite crutch.

Chorus:
The Planet guides me.
Lonely Planet guides me.
The Planet guides me.
It's all I need to know.

Where the cheapest thali's found.
Where to get my journal bound.
All the places A to Z,
To locate travelers just like me.

The Camel Club

AFTER FINALLY REACHING JAISALMER, IT WAS TIME FOR A BREAK. And what better way to rest the old backside than … to go on a camel safari.

Our group of twelve travelers (with Germany, Scotland, Ireland, England, Australia, and the United States represented) saddled up our camels and were guided out into the wilderness.

Camels have always been part of my romanticized picture of the desert: camel silhouettes at sunset riding atop massive dunes; the three wise men riding them in search of baby Jesus; Lawrence of Arabia; etc.

Forget it. Camels are the noisiest, smelliest creatures on earth. Dog breath is perfume when compared to camel breath. Their enormous pink bubble-gum tongues often hang out of their mouths in a long, low camel raspberry.

My camel, Buta, was in the habit of biting the butts of his compadres, so he and I were always positioned in front. This allowed me to gaze at the stark horizon, living in the illusion that I was on some sort of grand adventure, when in reality I was on the Indian equivalent of a pony ride at the zoo.

The first day of trekking went smoothly, aside from two of the camels bolting from the pack carrying a terrified Brit and an amused Aussie on a chaotic detour. Our guides cooked us a simple dinner of chapatis and rice, then excused themselves. Our camels bedded down before us among the sand dunes. We soon followed suit, pulling out sleeping bags and nestling down in brightly colored, fiber-filled clumps nearby. Under a blanket of a million stars, the conversations ebbed into silence.

Then, as if directed by some sort of cosmic cue or perhaps Mel Brooks, our camels began to simultaneously snort and groan and chew and belch and fart as if there was no tomorrow. (I can't imagine the three wise men ever having a serious conversation with these creatures around.) We tried to ignore it, but we were all soon laughing with disgust. We noticed our guides had made their camp upwind of our beasts of burden.

The next morning I was chatting with the head guide and asked what he had done before taking up life as a guide. "Worked in a bus station," came the reply. I said he must prefer working outdoors in the desert. "Are you kidding?" he said. "Working with camels stinks." I had no rebuttal.

After breaking camp and a few hours of riding we came upon a section of highway, and our "wilderness" journey abruptly came to an end. We had all signed up for the abbreviated trek. This is where we caught our bus back.

The bus appeared from behind a sand dune moments later, straining with the weight of passengers. We all opted to climb the ladder to the roof.

The ride was splendid. With the rough, sandy road, the bus couldn't go much over twenty-five miles an hour. Just fast enough to create a breeze up top.

Outside of Jaisalmer, the bus stopped and we were told to get off. Passengers are not allowed to ride on the roof within the city limits. After much adjusting, pushing, and cramming, we were all inside the bus. The last one on, Cora, had to sit on the driver's knee and help shift.

Our moods soured as the temperature in the bus soared. "What a way to spend Christmas Day," someone muttered. I looked down at my watch. I'd forgotten. Today was December 25.

With dust pouring in through the windows and sweat dripping onto the bus floor, I began softly,

"Dashing through the snow

In a one-horse open sleigh. ..."

First there were groans and I continued solo. But soon the Scots, Campbell, and Karen joined, followed soon by the rest of the camel club.

"Jingle bells. Jingle bells. Jingle all the way."

Most of the locals on the bus just stared ahead. A few shook their heads in disbelief, and the bus driver smiled broadly and tapped his foot.

We all laughed at the absurdity. Would any of us have ever believed we'd find ourselves packed on a bus in the middle of Rajasthan on Christmas Day?

The medley of carols continued. "Joy to the World," "Frosty the Snowman," and "Winter Wonderland."

When we got to "Away in the Manger," I couldn't resist and led the second verse.

"The camels are farting, the baby awakes.

But little Lord ..."

A Birkenstock sandal rapped me upside the head before I could finish.

The bus arrived back at our hotel somewhere between "Rudolph" and "Little Dummer Boy."

If I haven't put you off by now and you would like your very own camel, you can buy a good used one in India for about ten thousand rupees ($350). I forgot to ask if that included the limited warranty.

A Night in Jail

I WAS USHERED INTO THE POLICE STATION'S HOLDING CELL. ONE chair sat alone in the gray-walled room lit by a shaft of light split by the bars on the only window. This all looked a little too much like my memories of the film *Midnight Express*. "Your passport," said the stoic sergeant, and I surrendered it to an armed guard who disappeared around the corner.

Five minutes passed in silence as the sergeant inspected my bike, my gear, my helmet, and my water bottles. The armed guard returned with my passport. The sergeant gave it back, smiled, and said, "You may stay."

You see—I wasn't a prisoner—I was a guest.

When I arrived in Takhatgarh, Rajasthan, I had no intention of spending the night in jail. But after a group of fifty locals convinced me the only hotel was a den of thieves and drug pushers and personally escorted me to police headquarters, I didn't have much of a choice.

A flurry of activity ensued. A cot with an extra-thick mattress was carried into my jail cell along with a small bedside table. An extension cord appeared through the barred window. A guard plugged it into what I later discovered was their only television. I was informed the evening's meal would be potatoes with mixed vegetables and rice. I washed up and was served by the smiling in-house cook, who filled my plate with *alu mattar* (curried potatoes and peas, smothered in garlic) at the slightest sign of it emptying.

While I was enjoying truly one of the best meals I'd eaten in India, a knock at the door announced the lieutenant commander, who greeted me and marveled at my bicycle. He then pointed to my sleeping bag spread out on the cot and said, "You demonstrate."

I figured he wanted to see it displayed. So I took it out of its stuff sack and held the blue mummy bag up Carol Merrill-style, gesturing at the sleek and functional zipper.

"No. You demonstrate," he bellowed.

I obeyed. Setting the bag down on the concrete floor, I got down on my hands and knees, climbed inside, and zipped up the zipper. The commander began to chuckle. So did the cook. I then reached out and pulled the drawstring, cinching the bag around my face so that only my nose poked through. The entire room erupted with laughter. Several men in uniform were guffawing so loudly, they held on to one another to keep from falling over. It was at that moment I realized I was living a stand-up comic's dream: In India, everywhere I went I drew a crowd and everything I did was funny.

Later, as I slept soundly and securely in my cell, a loud rapping came at the bars, and I jumped up to a voice calling, "English TV, English TV!" I opened the door and one of the guards came bounding in and switched on the light and then the TV, cranking it up to full volume. He dragged the chair over next to the bed where I had returned, sat down, and grandly gestured at the twelve-inch screen. My eyes finally focused on an old black-and-white episode of Charles Dickens' *Great Expectations* with a young Michael York as Pip. The guard smiled, fully convinced I was delighted. I glanced down at my watch. It was 2 A.M.

I forced a smile—and throughout the entire two-hour episode, couldn't help but imagine the thieves and drug pushers across town … sound asleep.

The Bhagvati Binge

I MET BHAGVATI IN AN ICE CREAM SHOP IN BANSWARA, MADHYA Pradesh, and he invited me to spend the night at his home. A small, frail man with more-salt-than-pepper hair and a smile that revealed missing and tobacco-stained teeth. After thirty-five years he had retired from the railway service. He showed me the chair he'd occupied for three and a half decades, earning a top salary of two thousand rupees a month (about sixty-five dollars).

That evening we walked the streets and stopped at the city park, where several food vendors were set up around the perimeter of a large fountain. Bhagvati took me on a tour of Indian fried foods, sampling the dishes at each stall. And although I was the rich American, it was apparent from the start I would not be allowed to spend one rupee while his guest.

He asked which was my favorite dish and I pointed out the potato cakes with chickpeas. He took out a five-rupee note and ordered another large plate.

"No thank you. Really. I've had enough."

"No" was out of the question.

The vendor was proud that his dish had been selected for an encore and scooped out twice the normal portion. Bhagvati handed me the heaping plate and we sat down under the trees next to the cement fountain. Music blared from speakers whose woofers and tweeters had long since been ripped to shreds.

While contemplating how I was ever going to finish, he mentioned we'd be eating supper at the home of his dear friends, owners of the local sweet shop. Supper? I thought I was *eating* supper.

He walked and I waddled across town through dark, narrow streets. We passed several stray dogs sifting through garbage and a large group of kids playing tag around a parked bicycle-taxi. At one point, Bhagvati grabbed my hand. I was about to walk straight into a hole in the middle of the street large enough to swallow a car. No sign. No barriers. No need. The neighbors all knew it was there.

The concrete building we entered was plain and nondescript. But inside I was greeted by color, music, and wonderful curried smells. The apartment was filled with silks and tapestries. An altar to the elephant god Ganesh stood, glistening gold, in one corner, and a Hindi film soundtrack played through intact speakers.

Less than thirty minutes removed from my prior feeding frenzy, with my stomach already registering Thanksgiving fullness, I was served a large vegetarian *thali*. This plate of food looked more insurmountable than any mountain pass I'd ever climbed: crispy chickpea *papadams*, curried vegetables, saffron rice, lentils, fried pastry *samosas*, and pureed eggplant. I was handed a *lassi*, a thick yogurt drink, to wash it all down.

With mock enthusiasm, I dipped the fingers of my right hand into the rice and scooped up some vegetables. I chewed and swallowed and smiled.

Then Bhagvati dropped the bomb. He leaned over and whispered, "You must finish that and ask for more or they will be offended." I was stunned and began to sweat, not from the spice, but from gastronomic fear. Cyclists are known for their ability to pack away tens of thousands of calories at a sitting, and I have, on occasion, been teased about having two hollow legs. But this was too much. I prayed to Ganesh and Buddha and Jesus and any other religious being who might listen: "Please give me the strength not to give back everything this generous family has given me."

Unknowing witnesses to a small miracle, everyone watched as I placed the second to last portion of rice into my mouth (I had learned from prior experience that completely cleaning your plate is a request for more). Victory was mine.

Then our hostess entered with a platter. Sweets! I'd forgotten the sweets. The livelihood of this family and the ultimate insult if I refused. Couldn't Bhagvati explain I'd like a large box ... to go?

I picked the smallest of the large cream-colored chunks, as dense as Christmas fudge, imagining it as light and airy as cotton candy, and took a bite. My taste buds had ceased to function. It was just a clump of texture moving inside my mouth, scraping and grinding between my teeth and tongue. But I sang its praises in a muted voice.

I can't remember the next thirty minutes. I know I was asked several questions about life in America and of my impressions of India. I must have answered because the conversation continued. But every part of my being was focused on the Zen of gluttony. At some point I managed to slip that last piece to the family dog, to whom I owe my life.

After six weeks of cycling in India, the question no longer appears to be whether I'll survive the dangers and diseases ... but whether I'll survive the hospitality.

I Am God

IT HAD BEEN ONE OF THOSE DAYS—HOT AND DUSTY, WITH TRUCKS and buses honking. I'd had a couple of flats and I'd been run off the road ... forgive me ... I had "yielded the right-of-way" several times, thus swerving into several ditches.

To top it off, I was lost. Every map I obtain in India has its grand share of inaccuracies. So I'm in the habit of finding three or four different maps, all of the same region I'm traveling, comparing them all, and taking the majority opinion. But majority did not rule this time. Each map showed the road I was on branching off in a different direction.

The sun beat down on my lobster red arms. Not a scrap of shade in sight. As I considered throwing my chances (and my maps) to the wind, a teenage boy, dressed in a white, pressed long-sleeved shirt, long dark slacks, and sandals, rode up on his scooter. The intense whine of the motor of this one cylinder, exhaust-spewing excuse for transportation cut through all the rest of the noise on the highway.

He left the motor running and called out, "One minute of your time?" A harmless request, but I have learned that, in a country of 900 million people, if you give everyone a minute who asks for one, you soon run out of minutes.

In this particular situation I chose to be completely rude, withholding my sixty seconds of attention and pedaling off. Soon came the high-pitched scream of a scooter as the boy pulled up alongside me. "One minute of your time?" "Ignore him and he'll go away," I thought and picked up my pace. He caught up and began repeating, "Sir, I am talking. Sir, I am talking. Sir, I am talking." This went on for five minutes and I imagined with my luck, he had a full tank of gas.

I slammed on my brakes. "Okay, you win," I said. "You've got one minute," pointing to my watch. "Go."

He looked me straight in the eye, proudly folded his white-sleeved arms, and declared, "I am God." I was speechless. What is the proper response when a thirteen-year-old boy confides in you that he is a deity? "I am God!" he repeated more emphatically. What did he want? Did he want me to kneel at his feet? To sing his praises? Did he want my Visa card? *"I am God!"* I turned to go. "Sir, I am talking. Sir, I am talking."

I snapped. I lost my cool. I became unglued. I yelled at the top of my lungs, "Get out of my face. Leave me alone."

He stood his ground.

Bearing down on him, my face full with sunburned rage, I continued. "I don't care if you *are* a celestial being. Go. Be gone. Get thee the hell out of my life."

He took one step back, held out his hand, and said, "One hundred rupees."

That put me over the edge. Not only was he wasting my time, now he had the audacity to try and extort money from me. One hundred rupees for the privilege of not remaining in his company?

The entire day's events and frustrations soured in the pit of my stomach. "How many years would I spend in prison if I strangled him?" I premeditated. He must have seen the look of homicide in my eyes, for he quickly hopped on his scooter and scooted off before I could begin screaming again.

I straddled my bike frame, resting my cheek on my front handlebar bag, and looked out onto the ribbon of concrete bisecting the brown treeless landscape. Thank Krishna *that* was over. I worked my sandals into my toe clips and began to pedal. I didn't care that I had no idea where I was going. Anywhere had to be better than here.

A mile down the dusty highway I began to laugh. I laughed until tears came to my eyes as I realized what the poor kid had meant to say was, "I am *guide*." He had seen me with my maps and for a hundred rupees, he was willing to offer his assistance.

Now I'm not sure where he would have led me, but I'd gladly give a hundred rupees to hear *his* version of the story.

Back Roads
and Back Waters

A BICYCLE IS FREEDOM WHEN YOU'RE RIDING IT; IT'S A MILLSTONE when you're not.

With my bike on my shoulder, I waded into the river. In front of me trudged Avadhut, a seventeen-year-old boy, and his little friend, Babu, with my panniers perched on their heads. This is what happens when you attempt to navigate the back roads to Ratnagiri using a map of southern India (which is the equivalent of trying to locate Pike Street with a map of the entire Northwest).

Once across the river, all I had to do was push and/or carry my bike four kilometers along a footpath over the hills to a fishing village, where, if I was lucky, I could catch a ferry to another village where the road began again. All this was represented by a single unbroken line on my map.

I cursed the cartographer.

I should have known this was going to happen. I'd asked several locals whether I should continue along the coastal road. The conversations had all gone something like this:

"Is it possible to get to Ratnagiri on this road?"

"No. You must go this way."

"I can't get there via this small road?"

"No. That is long. This way is short."

"I don't care if it is long—I just want to know if I can get across this river."

"No. You must go this way."

"No? There is no way across the river?"

"No. This way is better."

And around and around it went. Locals don't comprehend that I want to take the "scenic route" and avoid all the trucks and buses. Because bikes only have one gear in India and are as heavy as tanks (they are called "push bikes," after all), most of my preferred routes are viewed as impossible.

So I'd gotten into the habit of ignoring advice. This time, though, my back road had dead-ended into a river.

Avadhut agreed to be my guide and after snacks and tea at his mother's, we set off on our adventure. We walked under groves of coconut, mango, and cashew trees occupied by monkeys and hornbills while discussing Hindi films and Michael Jackson. We stopped at a five-hundred-year-old temple in the forest where priests fed us pieces of coconut from the altar and blessed my bicycle. We shared a melted chocolate bar and a bottle of warm water. We joked with a group of tribal women out chopping and collecting firewood. We took a shortcut, a goat path actually, and how we got my gear-laden bicycle to the top of the hill without ropes is beyond me.

Five hours later, we arrived at the fishing village, bathed in sweat, filthy, and full of scrapes and bruises. After a two-hour wait for the ferry, I said good-bye to my new friends. I wadded up a fifty-rupee note and placed it in a film canister. I handed it to Avadhut and told him not to open it until he got home. I knew he wouldn't accept any payment otherwise. Then I boarded the ferry. (A *ferry* as defined in India is any vessel that floats and can carry more than one person.)

The only other passenger was an old peasant woman unsuccessfully trying to patch together a torn five-rupee note with her saliva. The old diesel engine chugged loudly, but I heard Avadhut call out one last time. A thought flashed through my mind as I waved—how much more of India would I experience if I got rid of my maps altogether?

Beached in Goa

THE STATE OF GOA IS KNOWN THROUGHOUT THE WORLD FOR ITS beautiful beaches and inexpensive beer—and for the first time in my travels in India, I felt hostility. The people staring at me all had scowls on their faces and foreign passports in their pockets. They were Europeans who had found their beach paradise and were obviously reluctant to share it with anyone. The few people who would speak to me had two things in common—they were in India because it was cheap and they disliked Indians. "They never stop gawking," said one man. I suggested this might be due to the fact he was naked and half of his head was shaved. He didn't respond.

I walked my bike past dozens of Enfield motorcycles and two-stroke scooters. I sat down at the top of a hill overlooking the beach.

"You shoulda seen this place twenty years ago, man."

His dreadlocks were the size of sausages and his face spoke of a thousand trips. The four teeth that remained in his mouth were gray on their way to black.

"Incredible. Before this place became popular, before it landed in the guidebooks, there was no garbage. Travelers respected the locals. You see down there. Twenty years ago, people never drove their motorcycles on the beach. They used to park 'em up here on the hilltop. It's a new breed of tourist, man."

Walter had left the United States and most of reality over twenty-two years ago. He'd since traveled the world, smoking dope and dropping acid. A month prior he'd been acquitted on drug charges in Thailand after three months in jail and eleven months on bail.

"I thought I was a goner. I don't like confined spaces. So I came here to celebrate. But they've gone and ruined it."

I offered him a bite of my chocolate bar.

"No way, man. That stuff'll kill ya."

I cycled south in search of a friendlier beach and found one. As I arrived, twelve men surrounded me, all asking if I needed a room. Huge packs of screaming children ran amok selling the daily newspaper for twice its listed price, and an intimate crowd of three hundred stood on the sandy shore to watch the sunset. A bit too friendly. The next morning I again cycled south.

That evening I sat in a small outdoor restaurant and looked out at the fishing boats as they returned with full nets. I had found my beach: a cove nestled between rocky hills with a small population of locals and travelers. A cool Arabian Sea breeze blew; the palm trees swayed. I positioned myself at a strategic table, visible to anyone who walked in, my nose not too buried in the trashy novel I'd picked up at a used-book store in a ritzy hotel lobby. I imagined a beautiful French or Swiss woman joining me for dinner and later walking hand-in-hand under a starlit night.

Then reality hit me in the form of a very large, bearded, drunken Englishman who collapsed into the empty chair at my table. "You look like you could use some company," he slurred. There was nowhere to run—all the other tables were occupied. He ordered four main dishes and six beers. "You know what's great about this country? You can get pissed seven nights a week for the same price as standing one round at a pub back home." My potentially romantic evening was spent listening to this man belt out Cat Stevens and Bread tunes in a three-note range that would have you believe Joe Cocker was opera trained.

I paid for my fish masala and studied my map. It was time to head inland. The beach scene was depressing me.

Oh! Canada

IT IS AMAZING THE NUMBER OF AMERICAN TRAVELERS I'VE MET around the world posing as Canadians. Being associated with a superpower isn't always a good thing. So sew a maple leaf on your backpack and all the world's your friend, or at least ambivalent about you.

I was therefore not the least bit surprised while traveling through central India that a local gentleman cycled up along side me and asked, "Canada?"

I had made up my mind to own up to my citizenship, no matter what the circumstances. "You're close. I'm from the United States."

"Canada?" the man repeated.

"American."

"Canada?"

"A little farther south. George Bush, Bill Clinton ... Disneyland. Any of those ring a bell?"

"Canada?"

I began to realize this was the only word in English this man knew. I smiled and waved. A couple of minutes later he turned off on one of the side roads.

"That was odd," I thought to myself. But this was India. Just the day before I had seen two men in the distance walking on the opposite side of the road. As I got closer, I realized one of them was naked. Not even shoes on his feet. The man walking next to him was clothed and carrying a jug of water. Less than five minutes later, another pair: two men, one of them older and naked, the younger man was wearing clothes and carrying a jug of water. As the fourth identical pair passed, I decided to flag them down and investigate. Fortunately, the younger man spoke English. He explained that the older men were Jain priests who, when ordained, take a vow of poverty, giving up all things material, including clothing. After a couple of encounters of this nature, the fact that someone repeatedly questions your citizenship doesn't faze you.

But over the next two days over a dozen people stopped me and asked, "Canada?" The first five or so were amusing. I kept looking at my bicycle to see if someone had slipped a Canadian flag sticker on one of my bags. I even took off my shirt and expected to find an "Ask me if I'm a Canadian" note pinned to it. I discovered only holes and sweat stains.

And why now? I'd been in India for over two months and nobody had placed me north of the forty-seventh parallel before.

Around day five of the silly-question fest, I lost it. I yelled at one man. "No, you idiot. Read my lips. I'm from the United States of America. The land of the free and the home of the brave." Then I sang "God Bless America" at the top of my lungs as he stared at me open-mouthed. After I finished, I made a goofy face and saluted him. He shook his head and walked away.

It took me a couple more days and a few more outbreaks before I discovered just who the idiot was.

I was traveling through Karnatika. The official language of this central Indian state is Kannada. K-a-n-n-a-d-a. Pronounced just the way it's spelled. The friendly locals were simply inquiring if the traveling cyclist spoke their language.

I wonder how you say "ugly American" in Kannada.

Ear Cleaners

"WANTED: PROFESSIONAL ROVING EAR CLEANER." NOW THERE'S an ad you won't find in the classifieds. These dedicated individuals roam the city streets, preaching the evils of earwax and practicing their art on anyone who sits down and, well ... lends them an ear. I didn't believe this occupation existed until there on the streets of Bombay sat eight men on park benches—smoking, reading the daily newspaper, and ... having their ears cleaned.

I was approached by one the other day as I stopped to fill my water bottles—a soft-spoken man carrying a little black case filled with large cotton swabs and dangerous-looking metal scoops and picks. "I am a professional and very gentle. See." He handed me a tattered, somewhat laminated certificate and smiled. It was written in Hindi, but I imagined it stated he had graduated with honors from an accredited ear-cleaning academy.

"No charge. I give you free inspection," he said and motioned me to sit on the ground next to a fruit stall. I pondered. I had been cycling the dusty, dirty roads of India for over two months. Why not? I sat.

He knelt down beside me and took an implement out of his bag. He moved in so closely I could feel the whiskers of his beard tickle my cheek. His breath smelled of tobacco and anise. There was a long pause. I began to panic. What was he going to thrust into my ear canal? I stood up with a jolt. "I don't think I can go through with this."

He stepped back in a gentle sweeping motion and displayed his implement of choice in the palm of his hand. He didn't speak a word, but his eyes and smile said, "You are a brave world traveler. How could you be afraid of a flashlight?" I slowly sat back down in the sand and then gave him a little go-ahead nod.

After some hems and haws came the diagnosis. "It is very bad. You have much wax buildup. For a very small fee I can remove it. But you have another very serious problem. You have stones in your ears. For a charge of only seventy-five rupees per stone I will remove them. In a hospital you will pay much more."

With all this excess wax, maybe I hadn't heard him correctly. "Stones?" "Yes," he said and pulled out a large pair of metal tweezers. "Don't worry. I'm a professional." The thought of him accidentally removing my eardrum propelled me onto my bike and down the street in seconds. I turned to see him frantically motioning me back while calling out, "Fifty rupees. Fifty rupees per stone."

I escaped what appeared to be a con job, but just in case I'll have my doctor take a long hard look when I get back to the States.

"Wanted: Slightly Used Denture Salesman." I kid you not. But that's another story.

Climb Every Mountain

THE SIGN AT THE FOOT OF THE NILGIRI HILLS IN TAMIL NADU had read: "This road contains several hairpin bends and steep gradients. You will have to strain your vehicle much."

My vehicle showed no signs of stress. I, on the other hand, was a virtual cycling fountain as sweat dripped from the end of my nose, my chin, my elbows, and my fingertips. For one stretch the road was so steep that for forty-five agonizing minutes I was forced to stand while pedaling to keep from falling over. They called these *hills*—the summit was at seven thousand feet.

I found myself panting out camp tunes from my childhood to take my mind off my aching legs and the thirty-six switchbacks.

> *Someone's sweating, Lord. Kumbaya.*
> *Someone's about to have a heart attack, Lord. Kumbaya.*
> *Someone's out of his freakin' mind to try and climb this mountain pass with thirty-six switchbacks in blistering heat on a bicycle with forty pounds of gear, Lord. Kumbaya.*
> *Oh, Lord....*

It didn't help much.

And I bet you're wondering, "How did he know there were thirty-six switchbacks?" No. I didn't actually count them. There was no need to. They are particularly cruel in this region of India, as each and every switchback is numbered and posted on a sign in the middle of the turn.

As I struggled with hairpin #19 and my sanity, I heard the whine of a diesel truck below me. It was traveling only slightly faster than I and it took until switchback #23 for it to catch up. A passenger leaned out the window and called out, "Why you not take the bus?" On the verge of tears I screamed, "I don't know!"

Another eternal half hour passed with no summit in sight and I battled with the thought of giving up. It would be so easy to get off my bike and wait for a ride. Then I began to hear the muffled sounds of drums and instruments, and through a clearing in the trees I saw a village perched on the side of the hill near the summit. Several bottle rockets shot into the sky. With newfound strength I sprinted to the top.

Smiling faces and laughter greeted me and I was instantly whisked off my bicycle. The local Brahmin priest walked up and gave me a big hug, and the villagers cheered. It just so happened this was the annual festival of the local goddess Kaliama, and I had cycled into the midst of it.

I was led by the priest to another part of the village where hundreds of people were gathered, and flung into the outer ring of a large circular dance.

Women in brightly colored saris of red, yellow, green, and orange danced together, and men in traditional dhotis whirled around me. Two weather-worn gents grabbed my hands and coached me through the steps. They were dressed in traditional dhotis, and I in traditional Lycra. With a mixture of adrenaline and exhaustion, bordering on delirium, I danced. My senses couldn't focus. It was all a blur of colors, firecrackers, incense, bells, and laughter.

Soon my legs began to buckle. It took several stumbles before my tutors realized that I wasn't a clumsy dancer, but on the verge of passing out. They led me off and gingerly placed me on a grassy mound, then rejoined the dance. A group of giggling children approached, offering me fresh bananas and coconuts. I gladly scooped up and partook of their offerings. One by one the kids plopped down and wriggled in close.

This couldn't be real. I had either died somewhere on the mountain pass or been plunked down in the middle of a National Geographic special. With my mouth full of coconut I glanced over my shoulder and gasped. Spread out before me was an exquisite view of the valley below (the home of wild elephants and tigers), where I had begun my climb. I'd been too busy struggling with the mountain pass to notice it before. I turned back and marveled at the celebration still in full swing.

A grin of pure emotion, mixed with exhaustion and exhilaration, spread across my face. And I once again knew what I have always known—the answer to why I didn't take the bus.

The Five Questions

WHAT IS YOUR NAME? WHAT IS YOUR COUNTRY? WHAT IS YOUR job? Are you alone? Are you married?

I have cycled over five thousand kilometers in India and been asked this series of questions as many times. The sheer repetition of answering can be a mind-numbing experience. On any given day, after fifty-some-odd inquiries, I begin to get creative to avoid boring myself to death. I become Hans, a professional speed skater from Austria. Or Bernardo, an elevator mechanic from Italy. Or Biff, a talent scout from Los Angeles.

These false statements don't eat at my conscience, for most of the people asking them are more concerned about practicing the few phrases of English they know than listening to the answers. I must admit, though, one very bright boy caught me with my cycling shorts down when he asked if I was a speed skater, why wasn't I at the Winter Olympics?

Adults are more likely to continue on to the more personal questions. "Are you alone?" is often misphrased as, "Are you lonely?" This poses a problem—for if I answer correctly, "No," they then want to meet the other members of my party, but if I answer "Yes," I send a little message to my subconscious that I am depressed.

Finally comes, "Are you married?" I can't win with this one either. If I answer truthfully, "No," it is immediately followed by, "How old are you?" When this is divulged, looks of genuine sorrow and pity come over the questioners' faces, since in the villages of India, I am long past the age of any hope of marriage. When I answer "Yes," the response is often confusion or outright offense that I would willingly leave my wife for such a long period of time.

If the conversation continues beyond "the five," I am usually asked why I am riding a bicycle. This is absolutely impossible to explain to someone who lives in a country where a bicycle represents economic status just barely above the destitute.

One afternoon a Mercedes Benz pulled off to the side of the road and the passenger, a man in a silk business suit, put up his hand, signaling for me to stop.

"Where are you from?"

"I'm from the United States."

"If you do not mind my asking—you are obviously wealthy enough to travel the world. Why do you ride this bicycle?"

"I wanted to see India and this is the best way?"

"Forgive me for saying so, but you are wrong. You could rent a car and a driver" (he gestured to his light blue Mercedes). "You could see much more of my country this way."

"But I really enjoy the challenge. The exercise."

"That is fine. You hire yourself a car. Then you drive to all the most beautiful places of India. Then you remove your bicycle and exercise until you are happy."

There was no need to continue this conversation. No argument would ever convince this man that I was anything other than crazy.

I thanked him for his advice. He returned to his car and the Mercedes pulled away. The look in his eyes and the smile on his face radiated his belief that he had changed my whole outlook on life. I had seen the light and would quickly pedal to the nearest car rental agency.

Unless I'm extremely rude and ignore everyone, the question-and-answer game will continue for the remainder of my travels. And whether I pose as rock star, a rocket scientist, or Rock Hudson, what does it matter? I'll always be a Westerner on a bicycle ... and therefore insane.

Arnold

IN BATALAGUNDU, A MIDSIZED TOWN LIKE MANY OTHER MIDSIZED towns in India, with bus stand, market, coffee and tea stalls, hotels, assorted cluttered shops, beggars, merchants, etc., I took a walk before sunset to snap some photos. While attempting to focus on a holy cow lounging in the middle of an intersection, oblivious to the dodging buses and auto rickshaws, I noticed a boy following me.

After clicking my bovine portrait I walked on, but I could see out of the corner of my eye that the boy was trying to get my attention. I stopped and he cautiously approached and asked in a formal, barely audible whisper, "Excuse me, sir. Do you know Arnold?"

"I'm sorry, I don't," I replied. "I'm just visiting here."

A look of shock spread over his face. "But you must know Arnold?"

Let's see ... the only Arnold I knew of was ... nah ... it couldn't be that Arnold. This was southern India.

The boy motioned for me to follow and he walked up the steps to his house. As I stepped inside the humble abode, his older sister ran giggling into the cubbyhole of a kitchen.

The main living room contained some small statues of Hindu gods and a large calendar with the electric blue portrait of Krishna. But by far the largest image in the room was a huge poster of *Terminator II*. It *was* that Arnold. The boy presented his cinematic shrine with pride and introduced me to his mother, who ordered her youngest son to round up some tea.

An awkward silence followed as the three of us sat beneath *The Terminator* sipping tea and smiling at each other.

"I have written to him," the boy finally blurted out, "but he does not write back. I think he is very busy. I have seen *Terminator* twenty-nine times and *Terminator II* over fifty. Arnold is the best actor in the world. Do you think you could deliver a message to him for me?"

I tried to explain that my chances for an audience with the Lord God Arnold were not much better than his own. I had never even seen Arnold Schwarzenegger in person, and the closest I'd come to rubbing elbows with a movie star of his caliber was once stepping on Clint Eastwood's toe at a celebrity golf tournament.

The boy tried to hide it, but I could read the disappointment on his face. The awkward silence returned, broken only by the giggling sister collecting teacups. Using the excuse that it would be hard to find my way back to my lodge in the dark, I made my escape.

I waved good-bye to the boy as he stood in the doorway, clutching his *Terminator II* cassette ... the best evidence I've seen to date that the world is rapidly turning into one big video store.

The Magic Word

BEYOND THE LOCKED GATE LAY A ROAD I DESPERATELY WANTED TO cycle; the highest in southern India, crossing from Tamil Nadu to Kerela through national forest land. The sign written in Tamil and English stated the road was closed to all vehicles. The frowning guard informed me my only option was to obtain permission from the regional director.

I knew the scenario. Back to Kodaikanal, where I would sit in a dank and dreary office for a day or two, only to be told the person I needed to see was away on business and could I please come back in a week.

There was one other option ... try some magic. In a similar situation, long ago, Ali Baba used the magic words "open sesame," but that was a different place and a different century, so I softly spoke the word "baksheesh."

The magic worked—the guard's face opened up into a smile, the gate opened up for me to pass, and my wallet opened up to produce twenty rupees. The guard pocketed the bribe ... I mean "tip" ... and waved me through.

I had promised the guard that I would cycle clear through the reserve in one day. But five kilometers down the road I came upon a cliff overlooking the aptly named Silent Valley. Up to that point I didn't believe that silence existed in India. For over three months my ears had been pounded by the din of traffic and humanity. It had become routine to insert my earplugs as I approached any city's limits. Even when I was out in the countryside, if I stopped for more than five minutes, I drew a boisterous crowd.

Now for the first time in over three months, and only by bribing my way onto a closed stretch of highway, I was alone. I leaned my bike against a pine tree. There was just enough room to lay down my sleeping bag. I breathed in the thick, muggy silence. Only the faint calls of birds and monkeys broke it. Nothing short of raging elephants was going to move me from this hallowed spot. I finally fell asleep after midnight underneath the gaze of Leo and Orion.

Rising with the sun, I set off after a breakfast of two bananas and a chocolate bar. The dirt road, pockmarked from annual monsoons and littered with rocks the size of softballs, wound up and down through pine and eucalyptus forest. It was more like riding a jackhammer than a bicycle, and I stopped near some cabins on the shore of a lake to rest my legs and my wrists.

A man in a green uniform came running up and demanded to see my permit. I gathered I was in serious trouble from his reaction to my lack of one. I was ordered to report to the chief warden immediately. A wave of anxiety broke over me. Would I be fined? or jailed? or both? Why hadn't I taken the National Highway?

As I approached the office, walking my bike, my fears suddenly melted away as I remembered the magic word. All would be well. I entered smiling and reached for my wallet.

Bent into Shape

LYING IN A SEMICONSCIOUS STATE IN AN EXPANDING POOL OF MY own sweat, I stared at the sky and wondered if my body would ever respond to stimulis again. Muscles I never knew I had ached and quivered. My condition had absolutely nothing to do with cycling; in fact, my bicycle had remained locked up for days.

Before my visit to the ashram in southern Kerela, my knowledge of yoga consisted of browsing through manuals with photos of people bent into positions that looked downright frightening. Was the human body really meant to perform like Gumby? Yet here I was in India attempting (without much success) the cobra, the locust, the plow, and the wheel. These positions, as interpreted by my body, could be renamed the pain, the torture, the agony, and the defeat.

Grunting and groaning along with me was an eclectic group of Westerners: Klaus, from Germany, was a serious practitioner, glaring at anyone who giggled or cracked a joke; Barbara, from San Francisco, had flown in for a weekend of emergency stress relief; Tom, from England, had found his calling and after three months was studying to be a yoga teacher; Sheryl, from Santa Cruz, had made the side trip to the ashram simply because it sounded cool.

The days were full at the ashram and the structured schedule left very little free time. Squeezed in between 5:30 A.M. and 10 P.M. were four hours of yoga (or asanas), three hours of meditation and chanting, two hours of lecture, one hour of "Karma Yoga" (otherwise known as chores), two meals, and two tea breaks. It all had the feel of summer camp, including a pristine lake for swimming (watch for crocodiles) and a corner café outside the ashram where you could often find desperate yogi wannabes sneaking a smoke or indulging in a large fruit salad.

The head swami, our lecturer and spiritual guide, was a Harvard-schooled Italian who had given up a career in international law to wear orange and pursue inner peace (he hadn't, however, given up his real estate holdings in California). His large protruding belly announced one of two things—he had ceased to practice yoga years ago, or he had a secret stash of cheese and chocolate in his room. I agreed with many of the concepts and ideas he shared and found some of his insights quite inspirational. But I must admit, I found it difficult to embrace a philosophy that suggests one abstain from both sex *and* garlic.

The peaceful surroundings, the healthy food, and the chance to exercise without sitting on a bicycle seat were a welcome break. After my week's stay, I don't feel any closer to true spiritual enlightenment … but I can touch my toes.

The Himsagar Express

WHILE SITTING ON THE SOUTHERNMOST TIP OF INDIA, WATCHING locals dog-paddle in the combined waters of the Indian Ocean, the Arabian Sea, and the Bay of Bengal, I pondered a problem. It had become too hot to continue cycling in the south. Fourteen liters of water had been converted to sweat during the day's ride, and I often felt I was melting into the pavement. The solution? Go north, young man, *way* north.

I had already booked and boarded the Himsagar Express before I discovered it wasn't. My journey north was scheduled to take seventy-five hours; the so-called express stopped at every other station.

I found my way to second class sleeper S2, seat #25, lower berth. The car's capacity was seventy-two, with each section sitting and sleeping eight. So many were the horror stories I'd heard about overcrowded Indian trains, yet as we pulled away from the Trivandrum station, I had the entire section to myself. "Travelers are prone to exaggeration," I thought.

Within the hour, after several stops, the car was completely full. Not only with passengers, but with boxes, crates, and burlap bags. Huge trunks with enormous metal clasps that I thought only existed in thick period novels were hoisted and stacked in every available corner. Three television sets, four sacks of rice, and a cage of chickens had found a home under a sign that read, "Less Luggage, More Comfort—Make Travel Pleasure."

"Is the baggage car full?" I asked a turbaned Sikh sitting next to me. "Only a fool would check anything of value onto an Indian train," he said. I discreetly tucked the claim check for my bicycle into my journal.

I imagined a couple of railway personnel going through the same drill as do flight attendants: "Welcome aboard the Himsagar Express. We would like to take a couple of moments to point out the only exit, currently blocked by a fat merchant who doesn't seem to have a seat assignment. All of the windows have been barred to protect your possessions from the hordes at our over one hundred station stops. In the event of an emergency, you shall surely die."

"You've got to be crazy to ride a bicycle in India," everyone had warned me. I gazed out the barred window, reliving my bicycle journey in a jerky stop-and-go-reverse as the train progressed northward.

Winding through Tamil Nadu, I came to the conclusion that Indian-style toilets, which already pose a challenge to Westerners, become downright dangerous on a moving train.

I watched as litter flew like confetti on the plains of Madhya Pradesh, thanks to India Railway's money-saving measure of not providing trash cans.

In Haryana, I learned never to stray far from the platform, as the train unexpectedly pulled away and caught me dining at a snack stand. I made the train, but arrived back at my seat wearing half my dinner.

I conversed with a Sikh while the wheat fields of Punjab blew by. His answer to all of India's problems? Get rid of the Muslims.

As we crossed the border into Jammu, a Muslim, having finished his evening prayers, confided in me, "You can never trust a Sikh, not one of them." So much for Gandhi's philosophy of tolerance.

Throughout the journey the scenery, the weather, the people, and the food changed. But one thing remained constant: the nasal dronings of the chai sellers, the tea-hawking mascots of the rail system.

In every state, at every station, and at any hour, they boarded the trains with piping-hot pots of tea chanting, "Chai, chai, chai." Half of my purchases were to quench a legitimate thirst, and the others were extortion-based. When someone hovers over you at three o'clock in the morning chanting monosyllables in a voice loud enough to wake the dead, it is amazing what you'll pay simply to get him to go away.

After three days, three hours, and thirty-three chais, I and my bicycle arrived in Jammu-Tawi near the border of Pakistan as a cool rain fell. I'm back in the saddle again.

A Shepherd's Life for Me

A TYPICAL HIMACHAL PRADESH TRAFFIC JAM CLOGS THE MOUNTAIN highway for miles. Not a vehicle in sight, just a thousand goats and sheep eating anything green in their path while being driven to the market town of Chamba by their shepherds. A shop owner storms out shaking his fist and cursing. A small battalion of goats has laid siege to his vegetable garden and taken no prisoners. A heated exchange takes place between shop owner and shepherds while this weary cyclist sips tea on the sidelines and enjoys, for once, not being the center of attention.

I have quickly fallen in love with this rugged state, shrouded in the beauty of the Himalayas and sprinkled with families of nomadic shepherds with their pillbox woolen caps and wide grins. Now, there's an ideal profession: work outdoors, travel, low stress, and all the free sweaters you can knit.

The other night as darkness fell with no town in sight, I pedaled up to a group of shepherds camped by a river and asked, in a combination of sign language and very poor Hindi, if I could share their campsite.

The eldest man nodded approval and I parked my bike, set out my sleeping bag, and prepared my dinner (four packages of stale tea biscuits and six bruised bananas). A little girl wandered over and stood staring at the stranger. I remembered a packet of balloons I had in my gear. I blew up a huge purple one and held it out to her.

It took at least five minutes for her to inch over the ten feet. But as soon as she had the balloon in her hand she ran giggling back to her mother.

Moments later I was sitting by a fire as an old woman with a face carved by years of sun, wind, and cold served me a huge plate of rice and *dahl*. Maybe if I was lucky, they'd let me travel with them for a day.

The last grain of rice eaten, the last dish scrubbed with sand and rinsed; one by one they excused themselves and bedded down. Where was everyone going? The night was young. No campfire songs? Charades anyone?

Disappointed and wide awake, I maneuvered my way through scores of snoozing goats to my sleeping bag. I lay back and gazed up at the sky awash in stars so plentiful I couldn't make out a single constellation. A young boy walked over, knelt down, and whispered, "Don't afraid. We with you."

The sky was still black when I woke with a start. They were gone. Only dying embers and goat droppings remained. Up the valley I spied flashlights beaming and heard whistles and vocal proddings as they moved on toward Chamba.

I glanced at my watch … 4 A.M.! After mentally crossing "shepherd" off my list of future professions, I pulled my sleeping bag up over my head and went back to sleep.

Jalori Pass

MY HEART POUNDED WILDLY AS THE BLACK CAR WITH ITS FLASHING red light disappeared around the bend along with several other official-looking vehicles. It had nearly run me off the road.

This hardly seems worth a mention, as being run off the road (yielding the right-of-way) can be a daily occurrence in India, and I have come to fondly think of the ditch as my second home. But this time there was no ditch, just a five-hundred-foot drop-off to the river below. And as guardrails have yet to become fashionable in Himachal Pradesh, if I had traveled three more feet, they wouldn't have found my body until spring.

I coaxed my heart back down under a hundred beats a minute, tried to whistle a happy tune, and continued on toward Jalori Pass.

Jalori Pass had been on my mind for over a week now. It didn't exist on one of my maps, and local opinion was running ninety-to-ten in favor of it being closed due to snow (if it did exist). But I had to try. Not just because it was there or because the summit was over ten thousand feet, but because the alternative was to backtrack a hundred kilometers and take a flatter, hotter, more boring route back to Delhi.

The muddy road climbed steeply through small villages, where I often heard the muffled trampings of runny-nosed Indian and Tibetan schoolkids as they ran after me in their oversized rubber boots, laughing and giggling. At times I could barely muster up enough speed to keep my bike upright. All sense of athletic achievement disappeared when a seventy-year-old woman passed me as she walked with a large stack of wood on her head. "Oh yeah, just wait till the downhill, granny."

I continued ascending, the temperature continued dropping. My wardrobe still reflected my journey in southern India, and although I was wearing every piece of clothing I presently owned, I still shivered. I put my head down and focused on the rocks in the road: their size, shape, and color. Somebody yelled in time to save me from braining myself on the bumper of a truck. It was on jacks in the middle of the road.

Three men stood shivering, all with wool blankets around their shoulders. Their transmission had frozen up on them, and they had sent their friend back to Delhi on a bus to get another. They'd been waiting nine days.

The men assured me that Jalori Pass was up there somewhere. But they didn't know if it was open either.

A couple of hours later, I found a man who could definitively answer my question—a trekking guide. "Sure it's open," he said while handing me a hot cup of chai, "you're only twelve kilometers from the summit."

He invited me into his tiny lodge, built to house foreign trekkers. A fire from a small wood-burning stove filled the room with more smoke than heat, but I wasn't about to complain.

"It has been a bad season. Everyone wants to hike in Nepal," he said while he placed another piece of soggy wood on the fire.

I held my throbbing fingers over the stove. "For weeks now I've been trying to find out whether this pass was open or not. Why doesn't anyone else know?"

"Oh, the pass has only been open for one day. The chief minister decided to take a trip and they just cleared it especially for him. He came through today. Did you see him?"...Yeah, I'd seen him.

So it is the chief minister I have to thank for my opportunity to conquer Jalori Pass. And if I see him in the capital of Shimla, I'll gladly shake his hand … right after I knee his driver in the groin.

Conned

HE WAS SO SMOOTH, SUCH A PRO, THAT THE MONEY WAS OUT OF my wallet and I was walking down the street before I had an inkling I'd been had.

As I remember, his first words were, "It's hot today, isn't it?" His soft-spoken demeanor stood out among the hordes of street hawkers and beggars. He owned a fruit export business and proudly supplied mangos and papayas to the U.S. Embassy. The spring in his step, he said, was due to his daughter's marriage, the following day, to an American from Berkeley. He offered to buy me a cup of coffee. He wanted to hear more about my bicycle journey.

As the sweet, brown brew arrived, he asked if I would honor his family by being a guest at the wedding. (This didn't seem so strange, as I had been invited to more than one wedding on my journey.) Also, he and his wife were going to see the renowned sitarist Ravi Shankar that evening, and if I gave him the money to buy a ticket, he'd get me a front-row seat. The next day, I would be a guest at their home outside of Delhi, and, if I didn't mind, he'd like to present as a gift to my mother a cookbook his wife had written ... and on and on and on. He was so charming and so believable that I forked over eight hundred rupees (twenty-five dollars) without thinking.

As I walked down the street the questions began to surface: Why had he written his name and address on a slip of paper? Every businessman, no matter how small his shop, has a business card. Why, if he was as wealthy as his business alluded, did he ask me for money to buy a concert ticket and a small, traditional gift for his daughter?

I began to feel really stupid. But this guy was so good I wasn't certain I'd been ripped off until I'd waited hours at the YMCA for him and his wife to pick me up. Of course, they never showed.

My reaction wasn't anger, but fascination. Having majored in acting in college, I was impressed with his craft. He never rushed, or got flustered. This man had put on a stellar performance for over two hours, not once breaking character. How many years had it taken him to hone his craft? I walked the same streets the following day. I wanted to find him in the marketplace again and applaud. Then I'd ask if I could follow and watch him work his skill on some other unsuspecting traveler. He may have seen me, but I didn't spot him in the strolling masses.

There is a temptation not to write this down at all and never admit publicly that I had been taken, duped, fooled, had. But come to think of it, it was a pretty cheap lesson overall. The price could have been $250 … or my bicycle.

What have I learned? Well, not to give money to a stranger on the spur of the moment. I know that! Everyone knows that. But isn't that the art and challenge of "the con"—to get someone to do something willingly that they know damn well they shouldn't do? If only I had told him I didn't have any money with me and I'd pay him that evening. But if I had been thinking that clearly, I would have seen through his lies and leaned over the table and said, "Sir. I'm on to you. How about if you pay *me* eight hundred rupees not to turn you in to the police." At least that's what I'd do in the movie version. In real life, though, I'm embarrassed … but also wiser.

Back to Delhi

CYCLING 112 MILES THE LAST DAY, I WAS LIKE A HORSE THAT SENSED the barn. A noisy, crowded, polluted barn, but one just the same. My trip had begun and would end with chaos. Highway 1 to Delhi was in the process of being widened to four lanes. Along certain portions they had paved but not yet opened the new section to traffic. It was the widest private bicycle path I had ever cycled. But an enormous stretch had not been widened at all, leaving a narrow two-lane highway of speeding trucks. I put my head down and pedaled into a stiff wind. A rearview mirror scraped my helmet at fifty miles an hour. "You are insane," I screamed to myself. "Get off the highway and take a bus." But the idiot, macho side of my brain screamed even louder, "I've made it this far. I'll be damned if I'm going to quit now."

I finally entered the city limits and the traffic slowed due to critical mass. After that last stretch and over five months and five thousand miles of pedaling, the intense traffic of Delhi didn't faze me at all. I was a veteran, dodging buses and auto rickshaws with the best of them, all while constantly ringing my bell to alert the jaywalking cows and pedestrians. I arrived at the YMCA tourist hostel exhausted but exhilarated. I'd come full circle, in an odd sort of way.

Sitting in the dining room, I spied brand-new travel guides perched on tables next to well-scrubbed travelers-to-be. I felt like a soldier, back from the front lines, watching new recruits preparing to leave. Their faces etched with fear and anxiety. And like an old war veteran, I spilled out stories and advice, requested or not. "Now that reminds me of an experience I had in Rajasthan…."

Back in my room, the fan attempting to whir away the ninety-five-degree heat, I imagined waking up from a deep sleep and opening the door to a cold haze of December—all of it a dusty dream.

So much to process. So much to remember. So many events that have subtly changed me. I don't feel changed or enlightened. The only things friends back home will notice are a few more gray hairs and a few more wrinkles (should have used more sunscreen). The other changes will crop up slowly, but they're there.

Many people have commented on how brave or crazy I was to cycle India alone. But I have long since learned to avoid being impressed with my own achievements. Consider a French cyclist I met on the way to Agra. He had already cycled twenty-two thousand miles on his trip: through Europe, across Canada and the United States, then from Alaska to South America. In Malaysia he'd been hit by a car and suffered two broken legs. He was flown back to France, where he recovered. He then got a new bike, flew back to Malaysia—to the same city and the exact same intersection where he'd been hit—and continued his journey. He'd pedaled across China, where he had to carry his bike over one pass due to snow. Then down through Nepal and into India. His plan after we parted was to cycle to Bombay, where he would catch a flight to South Africa and then cycle home to France. Oh, one more little detail … he was sixty-eight years old!

Now, I'm not sure I'll be able to accomplish such a feat when I'm that age, but I do plan to continue traveling and observing the world. And until someone convinces me there's a better way … I'll do so from a bicycle seat. Hope you enjoyed the ride.

South Africa

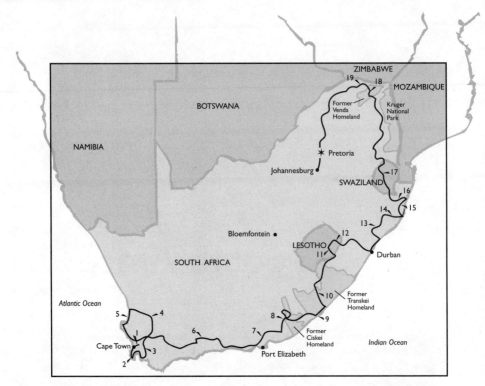

Bicycle Route ——

March 1995–August 1995

Map Key

1 First Flat—First Impressions
2 The Good Doctor
3 Beauties and the Beast
4 Another Hill
5 Flamingo Silhouettes
6 Carnivore
7 I Don't Wanna Grow Up
8 Fear and Hospitality
9 Shortcut—Long Haul
10 The Entertainer

11 The Mountain Kingdom
12 Seatless (Nowhere Near Seattle)
13 Another Saturday Night
14 Rugby Fever
15 Ultimate Chewy Toy
16 Swaziland Cowboy
17 Video Night in Venda
18 PJ and Farky
19 Dr. Travel and Mr. Home

My South Africa journey was the result of a survey and a song.

While in India I met fellow travelers from all over the planet. India rarely attracts the two-week-vacation tourist. When you meet foreigners with tattered backpacks and leather skin it is more appropriate to ask how many years they've been traveling than weeks. To these veterans of wanderlust I posed a simple question: "If you could return to one country you have visited, which would it be?"

South Africa won hands-down. Some cited the beauty, others the people and wildlife, but most couldn't give a specific reason. The country simply cried out to them.

This struck a chord with me. A year prior, my friend Laurie had taken me to a Johnny Clegg concert in Seattle for my birthday. Johnny is a white South African who grew up speaking and singing in Zulu as well as English. He and his band, Savuka, put on a concert that to this day echoes in my mind. Halfway through, the audience rose to dance and sing and never sat back down. As Johnny sang about South African skies, I swore that I'd see them myself one day.

After I had purchased a one-way, nonrefundable plane ticket, the warnings began. The U.S. State Department, guidebooks, and most of the people I talked to advised against traveling in the former homelands or in the townships. It didn't seem to matter that the rule of apartheid had ended and Nelson Mandela was now president following the first free elections. I was told I'd be safe only if I stuck to the well-worn tourist routes.

I told concerned friends and family I would heed these warnings, but deep down I knew my travels would take me beyond the secure boundaries ... and into the South Africa that Johnny had sung about.

First Flat—First Impressions

MY FRONT TIRE HISSED AT ME, AND I QUICKLY FELT METAL GRINDING on pavement. Only six kilometers into my South Africa bicycle journey and I had my first flat. The pessimist in me immediately projected ahead. "Let's see…," I thought to myself, "one puncture every six kilometers, divided by the total distance I've planned for this trip, means I can look forward to fixing 1,676 punctures." I leaned my bike against a railing on the #2 national highway leading from the airport to Cape Town and began the repair.

Cape Town is considered by many to be the most beautiful city in the world, but lift up its outskirts and you'll find the Cape Flats— a sprawling township composed of endless rows of tin and scrapwood shacks, thickly spread across a dusty, treeless plain. It was in the midst of that crushing sprawl that flat #1 occurred.

There was little to no traffic. The afternoon sun radiated off the large expanse of asphalt. As I dug for my repair kit, a tour bus stopped alongside. This bus had windows so large I could tell what brands of shoes the passengers were wearing. "I don't mean to sound paranoid," the driver yelled. "But you should get a ride into town. Bad things happen on this road, if you know what I mean. I've got extra room in the luggage cargo. I won't even charge you."

I considered his offer. The surroundings were bleak, but I'd seen worse. And there was something about putting my bicycle on a bus within the first hour of a grand journey that rubbed the adventurer in me the wrong way. "Thanks for your offer," I said, "but I'll finish fixing this flat and continue in on my own." He shook his head and gave me a "fine-with-me, it's-your-funeral" shrug.

The instant the bus drove out of sight, two black men emerged from the bushes and walked slowly toward me. "Great," I thought. "Thirty-seven minutes into my journey and I'm going to be robbed." I was a twenty-one-speed rolling Kmart: camera, dozens of rolls of film, binoculars, tape recorder, tent, sleeping bag, stove, tools, spare parts, and cash—a thief's Blue Light Special.

As the men approached, I hit my target heart rate without moving a muscle. Not wanting to look up, I focused on my tire pump and the task at hand, expecting at any moment for a knife to appear, or one of the men to jump me. They stopped two feet away. Keeping my head down, I tried to whistle something lighthearted, but only managed to drool on myself. "Oh, just get it over with, will you?" I thought to myself. But their feet in ragged sandals remained stationary. Finally, I glanced up and gave them my best disarming smile. There was a pause during which I thought about all the things I could be doing with my life other than bicycling in Africa. After several excruciating seconds, the two men smiled back, and then continued walking across the highway.

I breathed a sigh of relief. But with it came a flood of questions: Should I have accepted the ride? Was I going to spend the majority of my time in South Africa worrying about being robbed? Should I purchase some mace or a gun? Why had I so quickly jumped to conclusions? And finally, would I have reacted the same way if two white men had emerged from the bushes?

In the coming weeks, and the months that follow, I will have the opportunity to observe the new South Africa—including its problems, fears, and prejudices. But in doing so, I must also face my own.

The Good Doctor

THE DOCTOR FORCED ME TO GROAN AND BITE MY LIP, AND I CURSED him for it. He delighted in my pain and slapped me once again in the face.

I am, of course, speaking of the Cape Doctor; the name locals have given the relentless southeastern wind that blows all the pollution out of Cape Town and vicinity. Pedaling my way to Cape Point Nature Reserve, I didn't need an appointment to meet him. Typically the Cape Doctor is a phenomenon that only occurs during the summer, but this year it had unexpectedly lingered into autumn with a gale-force vengeance, at times making forward progress impossible.

What kept me going was the knowledge that I had a warm bunk awaiting me at the reserve's Environmental Center. A lovely woman I'd met arranged my stay there. I tried to call ahead to reconfirm the room, but the lines had been downed by the doctor.

I was cycling along a dramatic coastline. Below me waves tore at the base of Africa, and above a sheer cliff pushed into the sky. This little pocket of the world sports more plant species per square kilometer than anywhere else on earth, including the rain forest. I reminded myself to look up time and again to enjoy these wonders, but each time I did I received another slap from the doctor.

After hours struggling to keep my loaded bicycle upright, I arrived at a turn-off to the center and stared up at an 18 percent grade. My legs only functioned because I promised them, this would be it for the day. Rest and a shower awaited.

As I gasped for air at the top, the director greeted me sheepishly. Something was wrong. "You must be the cyclist." He began with the obvious, and after a few hems and haws, "I'm terribly sorry, but we are completely booked up with a scout troop and I can't allow you to stay." I responded politely that I understood. My legs wept.

I sat beside my bicycle, dejected, nursing a water bottle. It would be twenty-three kilometers to the nearest campground, and the sun was setting. A boy approached and said, "I talked with my scout leader and asked if she could make an exception. She told me she wasn't keen on having a strange man staying about."

Strange man, indeed! Didn't she know a bicycle was the internationally recognized symbol of the forthright, honest, and trusted traveler? Obviously not. I waved to a group of boys as I rolled back down the hill. This unfortunate group of scouts would have to forgo my skillful demonstration of the one knot I know how to tie.

I am presently bedded down for the night in the dirt and scrub, huddled beside a large bush that protects me from the ever-howling doctor. A little gray mongoose is staring at me and protesting my intrusion. I'll gladly put up with his insults, as there are four species of venomous snakes to be found in this park, including the Cape Cobra. Pleasant dreams.

Beauties and the Beast

LIGHT, AIRY MUSIC PLAYED AS TEACUPS CLINKED SAUCERS SET ON flowery table linens. Cloth napkins blossomed out of tall, crystal wineglasses. Seated for teatime at La Petit Ferme, with views of lush green vineyards, were the loveliest ladies of the Franshhoek Valley, dressed in fine attire and speaking softly in Afrikaans.

Driven down from the mountains to seek shelter from a raging thunderstorm, I sat, a beast among beauties, wearing the dirty polar fleece top I'd used as a pillow the night before while camped in the woods beside the highway. My cycling shorts dripped next to soggy shoes. Road grime clung to my unshaven face and the hairs of my legs. My perfume? "Eau de Road."

As a cyclist I try to avoid places with cute French names. These inevitably are dining establishments. Touring cyclists seldom dine, they feed. The goal is quantity, not cuisine.

I perused (and dripped on) the menu: "Rainbow trout de-boned and succulently hot-smoked—a specialty," and miles beyond my budget. Where was the cyclists' menu? "Healthy portions of peanut butter, tenderly wrapped in bread of wheat." Or "Chocolate-chip cookies, de-boxed, and served with four liters of chilled nectar of bovine." My decision quickly narrowed down to the one thing I could afford: tea and scones.

When my order arrived, I wasted little time appreciating the artistically arranged platter, and summed up the situation. If I cut each of the two scones into three pieces instead of in half, thus creating more surface area on which to pile all of the jam, butter, honey, and whipped cream provided, I could attain maximum consumption without resorting to directly spooning condiments into my mouth.

Moments before I attacked my plate, a plaque hanging on the wall next to me caught my eye. It read:

A day in such serene enjoyment spent
Is worth an age of splendid discontent.
Eat slowly; only men in rags and gluttons old in sin
Mistake themselves for carpet bags and tumble victuals in.

At first I smiled at staring patrons as I daintily scooped hundreds of calories' worth of sugar into my tea, making sure I held my pinkie high as I sipped. I gently wiped the corners of my mouth with my serviette after each jaw-stretching mouthful of condiment-laden scone. But soon the beast in me emerged, and I chomped and slurped and shoveled.

My feeding frenzy was interrupted by the exit of the four women seated at the table next to mine. I grunted farewell, wiping away misguided whipped cream from around my mouth with the back of my wrist. An eerie stillness came over La Petit Ferme as the beast, waiting to pounce, spied his next prey on the abandoned table—a perfect, untouched scone.

Another Hill

"YOU'RE THE FIRST BICYCLE TOURIST I'VE SEEN ON THIS ROAD SINCE we bought this farm," the man said, leaning on a spade on the edge of a tilled field.

"When was that?" I asked, wiping road dust from my teeth with a bandanna.

"Let's see," he began to figure. "That would be 1968."

The road through the foothills of the Cederberg Mountains came highly recommended by several locals. It wound through a wilderness area with towering slab peaks, once the home of the Sans bushmen, made popular by the movie *The Gods Must Be Crazy*. What the locals forgot to mention was this road was so rugged and steep that few of them would ever consider driving their own vehicles over it, let alone a bicycle.

My farm stop had a dual purpose: to ask for water and to stall, for beyond the plowed field was one of the steepest hills I'd ever laid eyes on. The farmer must have seen my lip quiver as I gazed at the cruel incline. "I can *baakie* you to the top, if you'd like," he said, pointing to the back of his four-wheel-drive pickup.

I have always loved climbing mountain passes. They're meditative. Long, slow, rhythmic ascents that last for hours. At the top there is a reward: a summit sign that screams, "This is it. You've made it. It's all downhill from here." Foothills, on the other hand, are just plain cruel. They demand as much or more effort from you than any mountain pass, and give little in return: no spectacular views, no elevation markers, and no summit signs.

Years prior, at the age of nineteen, I would have immediately declined the farmer's offer. I might have even laughed. The mere thought of accepting a ride was tantamount to defeat. Fifteen years later, I thought long and hard, with the words "Yes, please," poised on my lips. But my vocal chords malfunctioned and an inner voice confirmed, "Accept a ride today, Willie, and tomorrow you'll be touring South Africa in that big tourist bus with your bicycle stowed in the luggage compartment."

In place of a ride, I accepted a bag of dried fruit with his parting words, "You'll need the energy."

Shifting into first gear, I positioned myself in the middle of the road for the climb. (There was no need to worry about traffic; I'd seen one vehicle in the past twenty-four hours.) As I grunted and strained, a small blue fly played hide-and-seek in my nostrils and ear canals, while my rear wheel fishtailed, searching for traction. I could manage only two hundred to three hundred meters before my legs felt as if they'd combust, and then I'd stop and pant and check my heart rate, hovering at 210. At one point I gave up riding and began pushing my bicycle up the hill, but instantly found out that it was depressing and more difficult than pedaling. So it was back in the saddle, where I composed scathing letters to each and everyone who'd suggested this route.

At the top of the hill my adrenaline took over and I cheered. I yahooed. I would have yodeled if I knew how. "No *baakies* or buses for me!"

My celebration lasted only long enough for me to wipe the stinging sweat from my eyes. From my victorious perch the road descended sharply and there, across a tiny valley, lay another hill, the mirror image of the one I'd just conquered. In humble silence, I stuffed a dried pear into my mouth and began the slow, rocky descent. "Foothills," I grumbled. My day had just begun.

Flamingo Silhouettes

THERE WAS NO DOUBT IN MY MIND. THE MOMENT I SAW THEM A little boy's giggle escaped through my smile. Five seconds I'll never forget. A travel memory created.

At Elands Bay, on the west coast of the Cape, I shared a campsite with a couple of backpackers. Suzi was from New Zealand and Annie from England. They'd spent the last seventeen months wandering through Africa. Their tattered tent barely stood up to the afternoon gusts of sand-spitting wind, and mine nearly tumbled away before I could stake it down.

While we were planning yet another low-budget traveler's meal of pasta and S.O.S. (something on sale), our neighbors peeked over our wind-shielding hedge and invited us for dinner. We jumped at the opportunity, not only for the food and company, but for a look at their tent. This family from Pretoria had been coming to the same campground for thirty years. Their Barnum & Bailey–sized tent engulfed the entire site. I kept expecting a family of Lithuanian gymnasts to stroll out each morning.

The inside was palatial: large, thick mattresses, a dining table, stove, sink, and full-sized refrigerator. Fishing nets had been wetted and stretched to create a sandless floor.

We stuffed ourselves silly on barbecued snook (a popular local fish), wine, and bread topped with homemade jam. An evening of South African hospitality, including hugs and kisses good-night.

As we walked out of "Circus-Circus" and back to our humble domes, I heard muffled honking, and turned, expecting to see geese. I grabbed Suzi's arm as I saw the unmistakable silhouettes of three flamingos with their gravity-defying necks and long legs stretched, smoothly gliding across the moonlit waves.

My memory raced back three decades and I was holding my mother's arm while pushing the turnstile at the Sacramento Zoo. The day's goal was, of course, the monkey house and the bears. But first, always first, was a stop at the big concrete pool hosting the flamingos. "The zookeepers must paint these birds," I remember thinking. "Nothing is this color naturally—except cotton candy." I always got down on my hands and knees and looked up, making sure the few standing on single legs weren't amputees. And I wondered what they'd look like if they could fly—not old enough to understand their wings had been clipped. Then it was off to the monkeys, dragging my mother by her left arm, which to this day is two inches longer than her right.

That little boy never imagined that one day he'd see those amazing creatures while cycling in a distant country. The man he became is still giggling for it. I've since seen flocks of hundreds feeding in multicolored lagoons, but I'll always treasure that moonlit sighting.

Travel's lasting memories seldom come from destinations planned. They are found in fleeting moments and flamingo silhouettes.

Carnivore

VEGETARIANS BEWARE! SOUTH AFRICA IS A LAND OF MEAT EATERS; a carnival for carnivores; a land where butcher shops outnumber video stores; where "seldom is heard of bean sprouts and curd, and your arteries harden each day."

I have eaten more meat in the last month than I had in the previous decade. This on-slaughter of animal flesh began even before I "touched down" with a raw bacon sandwich served as a snack on my flight to Cape Town (three fatty slices on a bun with a paper-thin slice of tomato as garnish). I thought there had been some mistake until I witnessed another passenger, a high-school student returning home from a skating competition in the Netherlands, gobble his down without hesitation. The poor kid looked so hungry ... I gave him mine.

In South Africa, a meal isn't a meal without meat, and an event isn't an event without a *braai* (pronounced "bry"), or barbecue. At every corner store you can purchase beef pies, liver pies, mutton pies, and game pies (a pie stuffed with something you've seen on *Wild Kingdom*). In the region called the Little Karoo, you can dine on an ostrich burger and enjoy dried beef sticks the size of your leg.

I can avoid the cholesterol loading when preparing my own meals (although I did discover that the second ingredient in the soy pasta mix I fancied was beef fat), as there is always peanut butter and bread.

The real problem lies in the hospitality of the locals. I am often treated as if I were the prodigal son returning home, and the fatted calf is quickly slaughtered (or at least defrosted). A well-balanced meal is created not by adding vegetables, but by serving two to four other types of meat. In one household I was treated to the family favorite—beef and liver casserole. I learned in a college nutrition course that your body takes hours, sometimes days, to digest meat. This is fine if you have a leisurely afternoon planned, but I often embark on six to eight hours of activity minutes after eating a meal.

One morning last week I was invited in for breakfast at the farm where I had been allowed to pitch my tent. The two sons were eating large bowls of oatmeal with brown sugar, raisins, and fresh milk. Perfect. The youngest was in the process of ladling out my portion when his father entered, slapped his hand, and announced, "He'll have none of that. He has a mountain pass to climb on that bike of his. He needs a proper breakfast." Out came sausage patties, followed by bacon and eggs, all fried to stomach-seizing perfection. I watched longingly as the leftover oatmeal was fed to the chickens.

Despite the physical ramifications, I will continue to be polite and eat what I am served while cycling South Africa. Though I may need to take an extended break ... for a triple bypass.

I Don't Wanna Grow Up

HAD MY EARS DECEIVED ME? THE PICKUP TRUCK AHEAD OF ME moved slowly up the unpaved road, but I heard no engine. Was it electric, or simply tuned to perfection? I pedaled hard, passed, and immediately had my answer—the vehicle ran on grass, not gas. The owner had sheared off the front of the truck at the cab and replaced the motor with two donkeys, harnessed and struggling in first gear; a brilliant solution to high petrol prices, as long as he didn't mind shoveling exhaust in the city.

I continued on and pulled into a small store in the equally small town of Addo. The place teemed with people due to the holiday weekend, the anniversary of national elections and the launching of the new South Africa with Nelson Mandela at the helm.

Conversations buzzed around me as I packed provisions into my front panniers. But I could only enjoy the laughter, and the tones and clicks, for everyone spoke Xhosa (the *xh* is pronounced as a "click"). Soon after having stuffed an entire loaf of bread into a space the size of a tennis ball, I looked up to see five men surrounding me. One inquired in English about my bicycle. I answered the "How much? How far? How long?" trio of questions, and then asked one of my own.

"I have noticed a couple of young men dressed in Western suits with their faces painted a dull orange ... What does this signify?"

Instantly eyes looked away, feet shuffled, and hands dug into pockets. It was as if I'd vanished. The men continued speaking among themselves in Xhosa.

"Wrong question?" I thought to myself. Had I offended them? Should I apologize? Or should I simply get on my bike and ride away?

I turned slowly and reached for my handlebars. The tallest man stepped forward. "It is part of our black culture," he said. "When a boy wants to become a man he must…." There was a long pause, and a few of his friends snickered. "He must…." He shifted his weight from side to side and glanced up at the sky. Then he repeated a vertical chopping motion in the air with his right hand. His friends turned away and I spied shoulders quivering. "He must have his…." The chopping hand moved down toward his belt.

Bingo! "He must be circumcised," I blurted with game-show enthusiasm.

"Yes," the man sighed, with a grateful grin, as his friends burst into laughter.

The man further explained that the initiation was performed in the bush, with no painkillers and (one hopes) a very, very sharp knife. It was not uncommon for the individual to die from infection. This step into adulthood was the boy's own choice and only occurred when he decided it was time to become a man.

I thanked the man for tackling the extremely sensitive subject, and we shook hands.

"What is your name?" he asked.

I grinned … "Peter Pan."

Fear and Hospitality

"DO YOU WANT TO DIE?" THE SHORT, STOCKY FARMER GRABBED me by the shoulders and his eyes locked onto mine. "If you take this route you've planned to King William's Town, you'll be killed. Don't you understand? I know these people. The blacks...."

His voice suddenly dropped to a desperate whisper. Standing around us were his workers, all of whom were black. "The blacks are a different breed from you and me. Life means nothing to them. They'll kill you for that watch on your wrist. You must change your plans and go up into the Orange Free State. Here, I'll show you."

He grabbed my map and traced a route along the major highways clear to Johannesburg. It was a perfect route—for a trucker.

I thanked him for his advice, but said I'd prefer to continue along my chosen route. "You're a fool, soon to be a statistic." He walked away.

Fear is an unwanted part of my daily South African diet, a diet otherwise rich in kindness, hospitality, and natural beauty.

One late evening on the Cape I was looking for a place to camp. A middle-aged couple offered me a patch of their yard. I was invited in for supper. I sat down to a sandwich and a bowl of soup. Seconds later I noticed my hosts grabbing their coats.

"Oh. We already had dinner plans we couldn't break. Enjoy your meal." The door closed, then opened again. The woman poked her head in and said, "Oh. One more thing. Please don't rob us blind."

It dawned on me halfway through my sandwich that I didn't even know their names.

In the eight weeks I've cycled here, I can't think of one experience, one moment even, when I've had a good reason to be afraid. But every single day I'm reminded that I should be afraid. I'm constantly being offered advice: which roads to take and not to take, where not to camp, which parts of the country to avoid, to always carry a gun, to never travel alone—all of which relate to fearing people with darker skin than my own. As I ride along, I find myself balancing between caution and fear: Caution keeps you aware. Fear keeps you away.

I'm not one who thrives on danger. At Disneyland at the age of five I crouched in terror throughout the "Pirates of the Caribbean" because a friend had told me one of the pirates fired live ammunition. Of course, no bullet ever grazed my skin, but the suggestion that one might was enough to keep me at the bottom of that boat.

South Africa is far from Disneyland. Real bullets are fired here, as they are in every country on our not-so-peaceful planet. In the two days I spent in King William's Town, which lies on the border of the former homeland of Ciskei, four people died in an ongoing taxi war. (Taxis aren't regulated in this city, and when too many vehicles glut the market, competitors often begin shooting at one another.) This, of course, is the only news most white South Africans will read about King William's Town.

However, while I was there I discovered a community filled with incredibly friendly people. I was even given the opportunity to speak at a local primary school that only five years ago was for whites only. Of the group I spoke to, half were black. The headmaster was ecstatic that I'd come. "We don't get many travelers or foreigners visiting. It is even hard to fill teaching positions. People are afraid. Hopefully time will change that."

I'm presently headed toward the Transkei (another area I've been warned literally hundreds of times to avoid). And I often think of the farmer's comments. Perhaps I am foolish, but if the alternative is to become imprisoned by fear, I'll gladly remain a bicycling fool.

Shortcut—Long Haul

THERE IS NO BRIDGE OVER THE RIVER KAI. NO ROAD HUGS THE ocean along South Africa's aptly named Wild Coast. Inaccessibility has preserved its pristine beaches and abundant bird and marine life. For example, the distance between Kai Mouth and Wavecrest is a mere twenty kilometers as the crowned crane flies. But by car you must drive 75 axle-breaking kilometers along dirt tracks, or over 120 kilometers on teeth-shattering roads.

Two men seated on off-road motorcycles shared the small ferry as we crossed the great Kai River. Both of them assured me my best route would be the coastal one. "Take the shortcut," one man yelled as he revved his engine. "On a bicycle you should have no problem reaching Wavecrest by nightfall."

I took his advice. With a low spring tide, the sand on the beach was hard as a smooth asphalt road, and I effortlessly cycled along at thirty kilometers an hour. Fish eagles soared across cloudless skies and a school of three dozen dolphins played in the surf. "Forget nightfall," I thought to myself, "I'll be in Wavecrest by lunch."

That dream road abruptly ended as the sand turned soft, swallowing my front tire and nearly pitching me over the handlebars. I pushed for a while, then pulled, then dragged my bike through it. I was now progressing at an estimated one kilometer an hour. This did not bode well, for my shortcut had everything to do with the tide.

And with it now incoming, my sandy beach was quickly disappearing. I had to time the waves in order to slip past huge rock walls, frantically pushing my bike.

On one precarious stretch I thought I had it timed perfectly. But a second wave (they call them "sneakers") appeared out of nowhere, crashing ten feet in front of me. I managed to stay upright as the water surged around me, but it then slammed up against the rocks, changed course, and knocked me over on its way back out to sea. I spit out sand and salt water, struggling to drag my waterlogged bike and gear to safety before the next wave hit.

Soon the ocean had reclaimed all of the beachfront. My only option was to carry my bike and gear, stumbling along sharp, rocky cliffs and up steep sand dunes. My shoulders and lower back ached. Blood dripped from cuts on my knees. I was about to give up when I came upon a small dwelling, precariously perched atop one of the dunes. I was greeted at the rickety porch by "Knuckles," an old man with a sun-carved face. His two remaining front teeth held fast his stub of a cigarette that somehow managed to stay firmly lodged as he spoke.

"I thought you were on a motorcycle and having engine trouble. But this is a bike. What the hell are you doing here?" I showed him my map and asked about crossing the Kobonqaba River, the Xhosa name of which I had practiced for days, as it required a loud "click" to pronounce it correctly.

"Let me put it this way," he grinned. "With the tide in, you could stand on my shoulders and we'd both drown. You'd better stay here and push on in the morning."

I was wet, upset, and annoyed. Shortcut indeed. I swore never to take advice from someone on a motorized vehicle again. Then I glanced around and for the first time saw the view from Knuckles' porch. I'd been too busy struggling with my bike and gear to notice it before—the rugged coastline stretched out forever, an ellipse of blue that ebbed and flowed across miles of beach.

I laughed at myself. Why was I in such a hurry? Wavecrest was just a place on a map. I had no reservations, no appointments, no pressing schedule to meet.

I accepted Knuckles' offer and was treated to a glorious sunset while a full moon simultaneously rose over the Indian Ocean.

His humble fishing shack was built out of what appeared to be wood from old shipwrecks. There wasn't a plank that didn't have a gaping hole, gouge, or split. Every footstep sent out a chorus of creaks and moans.

"I used to live in the city. What a load of crap," said Knuckles as he served me up a bratwurst, then cut off a piece of his and tossed it to his stocky, short-haired mutt. "You work all your life and have nothing to show for it. That's why I moved out here. Look at that moon. With that, the stars, and the sea, I'm the richest man there ever was." He smiled and put on a pot of coffee. "Now what do you know of English football?"

Although I disappointed him on that subject, we swapped stories and swilled coffee late into the night.

The next day at low tide, with a belly full of eggs and brats, I waded across the Kobonqaba River three times—twice with gear, and finally with my bicycle carried above my head. I arrived at Wavecrest a full day later than planned. My shortcut had turned into a long haul, and it no longer bothered me in the least.

The Entertainer

I AWOKE TO THE SOUND OF FOOTSTEPS CRUNCHING ACROSS FROSTY grass. The unshaven face of Milton, a seventy-eight-year-old Xhosa farmer, appeared in the mesh window of my tent. I unzipped the flap. He knelt down and pointed off into the distance.

His voice was high pitched, yet resounded in raspy tones from his chest. A South African version of Yoda. "You see those mountains. Those mountains, over there. That is Ugi. *That* is Ugi. You do not want to travel that road. There are naughty boys on that road."

I asked Milton what he meant by naughty.

He made a gesture with his thumb. "They'll slit your throat."

I thought, "I don't know about you, Milton, but on my own personal naughty scale, slitting someone's throat ranks at least an eight."

I wanted to travel to Ugi simply because the tiny road on my map, a thin red squiggle that appeared to have been drawn by a first-grader on caffeine, intrigued me.

Milton's alternative route would take me through Umtata, the largest city in the Transkei. If I was going to get mugged, I reasoned, it was going to be there. But no matter how I stated my case, Milton wasn't going to let me leave his farm until I promised I'd take the "safer" route he'd prescribed.

So, in the long run, I lied to the man and his family who had generously fed me and let me camp next to their modest home. I promised to proceed via Umtata as I waved good-bye, but later took the turn-off toward Ugi instead.

The single-lane dirt road wound through tribal farmland. Far off in the distance the Drakensburg Mountains and Lesotho loomed.

It was obvious there would be few opportunities to purchase food, so when the tiny road bisected a larger highway, I searched for a store. A gust of wind sent clouds of dust and plastic bags whirling against tin shacks and gutted cars. Vehicles maneuvered around huge potholes and clusters of people wrapped in winter blankets shuffled about as I pedaled up. I waved a friendly greeting—the only smile in return hung twenty feet in the air on a billboard announcing a new and improved laundry soap. "Gets even fatty stains out," the woman beamed.

The store personnel glared as I perused the half-empty shelves, selecting a carton of long-life milk, two oranges, and an apple. As I searched my pockets for money, I noticed a crowd begin to gather. By the time I exited the store, three tough-looking young men stood, arms folded in front of their chests, blocking the path to my bicycle.

I decided to stall. Maybe everyone would get bored and go home. I peeled an orange and felt very foreign, and very alone. I ate the second orange. No one moved. I ate the apple, core included. Some more people gathered around. Still not a smile. Not a word.

I came to the realization that the next move in this stand-off was mine. I slowly walked toward my bicycle. As I approached, the three men stepped aside just enough to let me squeeze by. I wasn't sure if the hairs on my neck were standing up because of the warning Milton had given me or because my survival instinct was telling me to do something, fast. I reached into the pocket of one of my panniers and felt for the only security measure I had for this type of situation. I spun quickly around to face the crowd … and began tossing beanbags in the air.

I learned to juggle in high school while on the tennis team. As the last alternate on the B squad, I spent most of my time sitting courtside, waiting for someone to pull a hamstring. And as tennis is not an injury-prone sport and as there are three tennis balls to a can, my skill developed out of sheer boredom.

My impromptu South African performance would not have secured me a job with Barnum & Bailey, but it was executed with enthusiasm and conviction: the Lazy Man's Juggle, the Helicopter, behind my back and under my legs. I was too intently focused on not dropping the bags to notice if anyone was amused. But I was still alive, that counted for something. For my finale I threw one bag high in the air, crouched at the last second, and caught it in the nape of my neck. Then, with a quick whiplash snap, I sent it skyward, and caught it in my baseball cap.

The crowd, which had tripled in size, cheered and clapped. The tension had melted away and I faced a crowd full of smiles and grins. The three formerly menacing gentlemen, whom I'd imagined were going to leave me for dead in a ditch somewhere, patted me on the shoulders and asked me where I was from and where I was going. And when they found out I was from the United States ... they asked me about the O. J. trial.

It was the one thing I truly gloated about before I left Seattle. Not that I was going to travel for months in some far distant land. Not that I was going to see herds of wild animals and dance in the African moonlight. It was that I would not have to be subjected to one more minute of the tabloid trial of the century. But thanks to CNN and satellite technology, O. J.'s fate was being discussed on an obscure back road of tribal Africa.

After an encore juggling performance I cycled out of town. I glanced over my shoulder and watched the waving crowd disappear in a cloud of dust and plastic, ever so thankful I'd never mastered the game of tennis.

The Mountain Kingdom

THE GLASSY-EYED BORDER OFFICIAL PUSHED THE STAMP DOWN firmly on the ink pad and then smacked it onto my open passport. Nothing. It was too cold for the ink to stick. He breathed alcohol-soaked breath on the stamp in an attempt to warm it up and then tried again. Same result. Finally, with the help of a cigarette lighter, he managed to produce a barely intelligible, upside-down entrance stamp in my passport. Welcome to Lesotho—the Mountain Kingdom.

What had possessed me to take this monstrously steep detour from my bicycle journey through South Africa up to a country whose lowest elevation was about five thousand feet? Cultural curiosity? Global awareness? Nothing so high minded. The simple fact was Lesotho contained within its borders the highest mountain pass in southern Africa and as a cyclist, I wanted to climb it. My only obstacle, an ominous one, was winter. It was fast approaching. Numerous were the stories I'd collected from fellow travelers who'd been snowbound for weeks on ill-timed journeys to Lesotho. Even in the summer months, January through March, temperatures can fall below freezing.

My first concern as I crossed the border was shelter. The sun was sinking as fast as the temperature, and at eight thousand feet, I knew I'd spend a frigid, sleepless night in my flimsy tent. But where? The road ahead wandered through barren mountains.

An hour later, with a tightly woven Basotho blanket wrapped around my shoulders, I stood outside a hut in the tiny village of Hamonyane. Several children, oblivious to the cold, danced around me in their underwear. I didn't know how to say, "Are you crazy? Get some clothes on," in Sesotho, the local language, so I remained silent, watching the sun set behind an awesome curtain of jagged peaks. As the darkness crept up the deep river gorge, I became aware of a thousand stars in the sky—and a million goose bumps on my bare legs. Friendly voices called me in for supper.

I was the guest of Joseas. We'd met on the side of the road shortly after I'd crossed the border and, after he convinced the chief of the village I was not in search of a wife, permission to overnight was granted. Joseas is a grandfather at thirty-nine. His kind face has been spared the lines and wrinkles one would expect from the hard life of the gold mines. There is no work in Lesotho, so for twenty years he has traveled to the mines in neighboring South Africa: twelve months of mining followed by a fifty-six-day leave to visit his family and home.

We sat down to a dinner of sheep's heart, lung, and intestine, prepared over a cow-dung fire by his wife and mother-in-law. As the honored guest, I was awarded the largest slabs of fat. I managed to smile while my stomach turned somersaults.

As we readied for bed, children's voices could be heard singing from a neighboring hut. I asked Joseas what the song meant. "The lyrics talk of how the rest of the world sees Lesotho as a tiny kingdom. But we think it is big because it is rich in mountains, water, and cattle."

I fell asleep under three heavy blankets and the spell of the magical melody.

The next morning, after many cups of tea to chase away the morning chill, we hiked down into the river gorge. Our conversations echoed back as Joseas led me through the caves where shepherd boys sheltered their sheep and cattle during winter storms.

"How many days left in your leave?" My question bounced all around us.

"Thirty-three," he sighed.

Back at the village, a squadron of nine boys and three dogs waited to guide me back to the road. Joseas and I shook hands, then embraced.

"I hope a time comes soon when you can watch the seasons change in your own country," I said. "But for now I wish you thirty-three more splendid days in the mountain kingdom you call home."

Joseas smiled and wiped away a tear. I turned and began pushing my bike up the path.

During the next five days I struggled along roads with gravel the size of bowling balls. Highway construction in this part of the world seems to consist of rolling large rocks down mountainsides. When a sufficient number has collected, they declare it a "road." The locals wisely use ponies.

As I passed small villages I greeted the women with "*khotso*" (peace), the *k* pronounced as if expectorating phlegm. The men were greeted with "*ndade,*" pronounced with a roller coaster of pitch and intonation, which means "father" in Sesotho. Kids surrounded me, giggling and dancing around my bicycle, some bravely approaching close enough to "pet" it.

I pedaled along, feeling as if I was the first Westerner to venture there. This "explorer" mystique shattered minutes later as I heard a small voice from the heavens, "Gimmee some sweeeeets." I looked up to see a little speck of a shepherd boy, a thousand feet up the mountainside, frantically waving and calling, the phrase, no doubt, learned from tourists or international aid workers.

Each morning I'd wake up shivering in a shelter or hut and wonder if the gathering clouds would lay down an unwanted blanket of snow. I was quickly reaching the limits of my physical and mental endurance.

My less-than-expeditionworthy map had left out a few mountain passes here and there. Coming around a corner expecting to see a pristine valley to coast through and discovering yet another seven-to-ten-mile pass to climb was devastating. Tears of frustration mixed with cold, salty sweat.

In the middle of one of these climbs I'd had enough. I lay in a ditch next to my heavily laden mountain bike, my legs quivering, and vowed to wait for a bus. This was the onset of delirium, as I had not encountered a single vehicle in over two days. I struggled back onto the road.

I made it to the top and discovered a small roadside settlement. An old Basotho woman beckoned me into a large windowless thatched-roof hut with a gesture and a smile. I hesitated, but she grabbed my hand and led me inside. I stumbled blindly, like a late moviegoer entering a darkened theater. My ears heard music and laughter. My nose smelled wood smoke and pungent sweat. My skin sensed bodies swaying and twirling. My eyes saw nothing.

I had entered a *shebeen*, a local drinking and dancing establishment, and I'd lost hold of my elderly date. With my hands outstretched, protecting my face from large, solid objects, I made my way slowly toward the music. Live or recorded? I couldn't tell. My hands made contact with flesh. There was a yelp and all percussion ceased. I had my answer. I'd nearly thumbed the drummer in the eye.

Light flooded the *shebeen* as someone opened the door and many patrons became aware for the first time that there was a foreigner among them.

I apologized to the drummer. His one, waist-high drum was made of sheepskin stretched over a cylindrical wooden frame. Several pieces of metal, strung through coat-hanger wire, were positioned so he could hit them on both the up and down strokes, for a muffled cymbal effect. I shook hands with the other half of the band, the squeeze-box player.

A strong hand grabbed my shoulder and spun me around. An old tin can was thrust at me, and all eyes watched as I accepted it. I wasn't sure whether to drink the contents or ceremoniously sprinkle them over my head and feet. Then it dawned on me. This one was "on the house," and I took a hesitant sip. The crowd laughed at my facial reaction to the lukewarm, bitterly sour, gritty liquid that bore no resemblance to the beer it was supposed to be.

Then the band struck up a tune that struck my ears as Cajun with a tribal beat. My dance card filled. Everyone, male and female alike, wanted to boogie with the American. My dance partners all had Lesotho's harsh mountain climate etched on their faces, but here it was warm, and all blankets and concerns had been checked at the door.

After buying a round for the band, I emerged squinty eyed and rubbery legged back out into what remained of a winter's day. My progress had been painfully slow in Lesotho; I'd struggled to cycle 150 kilometers in five days along the rugged mountain roads. But the beauty of this mountain kingdom and the joy and friendship shared with me by its people had diluted my goal.

Reaching the top of southern Africa's highest mountain pass no longer seemed important.

A car pulling a trailer pulled up as I pushed my bike back onto the road. Familiar accents spilled through the windows—fellow Americans. They had driven the entire length of Lesotho on the main highway in one day. I got the feeling they were on the "seventeen-African-countries-in-fourteen-days" tour. They spoke of the vistas I'd missed and some roadside parks, then quickly rolled up their windows and zoomed off toward the South African border.

I shook my head, not the least bit envious. True, they had seen more of Lesotho in a single day ... but I had experienced more of Lesotho in a single hut.

Seatless
(Nowhere Near Seattle)

I WILL ADMIT, AS I'M SURE WILL THOUSANDS OF OTHERS, TO AN ongoing love affair with the bicycle. It has been my constant companion over fifty thousand kilometers of travel. I have yet to meet anyone, though, who will sing praises of the bicycle seat. Far from it. The most hated of bicycle parts, it makes life miserable—rubbing, chafing, bruising. It is, in layman's terms, a royal pain in the butt. I have often wished I could cycle without sitting on one. Last week my wish came true.

It was a cloudless day in Kwa Zulu Natal. I had camped the previous night with some archaeologists at a remote dig on the banks of the Tugela River. As I pedaled, my mind brimming with stories of the prehistoric inhabitants of Zululand, there was a loud crack. My seat pitched forward.

Upon inspection, I discovered the two bolts holding the seat to the post had snapped. Not a problem. I opened my front pannier and reached for my tools. My hand fished around, only coming in contact with dirty socks and a box of cookies. Tools were nowhere to be found. Big problem. Had I lost them or had they become part of the South African wealth redistribution program? Lost or stolen, it didn't matter. They were gone.

I looked around at the brown hills dotted with brown thatched huts. The odds of finding a six-millimeter Allen wrench were slim.

There I stood performing a touring cyclist's Shakespeare. I pondered my detached bicycle seat held high in one hand, as did Hamlet with the skull of his friend Yorrick, and with dramatic flair I proclaimed, "Alas, poor saddle. I knew it well."

No one applauded my soliloquy. Two white-chested ravens, my only audience, cawed their disapproval. It was time to get this tragicomedy on the road. So, for the next twenty-five kilometers of hilly gravel roads, I stood and pedaled.

As I panted and grunted, I couldn't decide whether the local Zulu tribespeople were laughing because I was a foreigner on a bicycle or because I was a foreigner on a bicycle without a seat. A couple of times my memory lapsed and I habitually sat down, only to be painfully reminded that my once-cursed friend was missing.

My arms, my legs, my neck, and my back ached after hours of what can only be described as the stair-climber workout from hell. Finally, I came upon a roadside repair station, temporarily set up to maintain construction vehicles. The necessary tools were found and I bolted my seat back to its rightful place. After tea with the head mechanic, I was on my way again.

The road climbed steadily, rising high above the Tugela Valley. After ten kilometers I reached the summit and began the long, slow descent. And with glorious pleasure … I sat. Unlike Hamlet's buddy, my friend had been resurrected, and I vowed never to take him for granted again.

Another Saturday Night

TIRED OF THE SAME OLD SATURDAY-NIGHT ROUTINE—GOING TO the theater, out for dinner and a movie, staying home and watching a video? Ready for a change? How about spending the night camped out on the floor of the Tip-Top Auto Garage outside of Ulundi, South Africa, sheltering from thundershowers? Sound intriguing? Then you may be ready for the life of a long-distance bicycle traveler.

Yes, I had other options. For instance, I could have stayed at the Holiday Inn in Ulundi, where my room would have been clean and sterile, the staff apolitical, and the only lasting memory ... a readout on my credit-card statement.

But I chose the Tip-Top. The owner, Joseph, waved as I pedaled up, and I asked him if I could pitch a tent nearby. He offered his hand in greeting and his garage for cover. Other "guests" had preceded me, as the repair station had no door. I cleared a place for my sleeping bag among goat droppings and nesting chickens.

A couple of locals stood in the corner swigging beer from tall liter bottles and talking politics. Holding a huge mug of sweet, brown coffee brewed for me by Jerico, one of Joseph's wives, I joined in the discussion. I only had to ask one question. "What do you think of President Mandela?" (Ulundi is the headquarters of the Inkatha Freedom Party, or IFP—the bitter and sometimes violent rival to Mandela's ANC.)

I never spoke another word. Curses flew and beer dribbled on unwiped chins. Predictions of chaos, secession, and civil war were accompanied by waving arms and stamping feet. Accusations mounted as bottles emptied.

Enough of politics. It was time for some entertainment. Joseph and his family and friends had never seen a tent before, so I bet Joseph I could set mine up in under five minutes. The crowd watched in wonder and then cheered as my freestanding dome stood functional in two minutes, forty-two seconds. (My personal best is one minute, thirty-four seconds while under siege by blackflies in northern Canada.)

Throughout the evening troubled motorists would wander into the garage, assume I was the owner (due to my white skin), and go into lengthy explanations in Zulu of car or mini-bus problems. I'd shake my head and point to my sleeping bag as if to say, "I only sleep here," and Joseph would laugh and come to the rescue.

It grew late and neighbors and other onlookers finally left. Joseph asked his son to go to their house next door and get me a drink. The little boy appeared five minutes later, walking ever so slowly, his eyes transfixed by the glass. Laughter filled the garage. The boy had filled a ten-ounce glass to the absolute brim with whiskey. I only joined in after it had been made clear I wasn't required to drink it all.

One by one family members excused themselves. "Good-night, Willie. Good-night, traveler. Good-night, white man."

Joseph was last. "Good-night, my friend."

I wrote in my journal and then blew out the candle, falling asleep to the sound of clucking chickens and rain dancing on the tin roof.

Another Saturday night on the road.

Rugby Fever

IT WAS THE DAY SOUTH AFRICA STOOD STILL. FROM CAPE TOWN to Jo'burg, life was put on hold while in pubs, stores, and homes, the masses watched the big event. Super Bowl Sunday paled in comparison. It was closer in magnitude to watching Neil Armstrong walk on the moon. The Springboks had made it to the finals and were playing New Zealand to decide the winner of the World Cup of Rugby.

I witnessed the spectacle crushed between seventy-five other beer-drinking, biltong-chewing fans at the rugby club in Hluhluwe (lisp twice and you've pronounced it correctly). I say "other fans" for I too was one.

When I arrived in South Africa I didn't know the difference between a scrum and a try. But I soon learned, for the country had a collective case of rugby fever. Every product endorsed it. Every newscast covered it, and every conversation got around to it. Infection was inevitable.

It began when I delayed my trip to Lesotho by a day to watch the opening match against Australia. I cycled up to a pub in the early afternoon.

"Get in here. The game is about to begin," someone yelled at me. "Don't bother with lockin' your damn bike. Bring it inside."

I squeezed into the already packed establishment.

A man with Popeye's arms and Whimpy's belly yelled over the crowd as he brought me a pint, "Are you from Germany? Switzerland? No. No. England?"

"I'm from the United States."

"Aw, Christ. Then you don't know rugby, do you? Just that sissy game where they wear all the pads. Well. Come over here and sit and watch. I'll buy your beers as long as you don't root for the Aussies."

South Africa upset the favored Australians and the fever set in.

In the coming weeks I cycled hours out of my way to find a TV so I could watch South Africa advance. One game I even feigned visiting a relative at a retirement home so I could watch the match against Japan on the nineteen-inch color screen in their lounge.

I had managed to make it to the Hluhluwe Rugby Club for the final match thanks to Andre and Alan, two big-bellied fishermen who gave me a lift from the TV-less False Bay Nature Reserve.

South Africa had been barred from the first two World Cups due to apartheid. Few South Africans ever dreamed they'd witness a black president wearing a Springbok cap and jersey, greeting players on the field, or that they'd see a colored man (Chester Williams) star in the traditionally all-white sport.

Regulation time ended with the score tied and, for the first time in rugby history, a game went into overtime. Our barkeep went into overdrive. The volume of excitement began to rise at the Hluhluwe club—a dull roar of feet stomping and hands slapping tabletops, punctuated with groans for missed kicks and cheers for defensive tackles. South Africa scored, bringing everyone to their feet. With two minutes remaining the roar dwindled to silence as everyone stared at the screen and prayed for the clock to run out. The barkeep even stopped pouring.

The tension broke as the official blew his whistle. The game was over. South Africa had won. The crowd erupted and the walls shook from cheers, yells, laughter, and singing. I found myself hugging burly men I'd never met and dancing silly jigs with my fingers in my ears to prevent permanent hearing loss.

After twenty minutes of unrelenting celebration I noticed a woman sitting in the corner with a somber look on her face. I approached and asked with a shout why she looked so sad. Had she been rooting for New Zealand?

"No," she replied, lifting up a small South African flag on a stick.

"Then why the long face?"

"It's over."

"Yes, but you won."

"You don't understand. Now that the World Cup is over … it's back to talking politics."

Ultimate Chewy Toy

A PIECE OF ADVICE. IF YOU ARE TRAVELING TO SOUTH AFRICA specifically to visit its wondrous game reserves … leave your bike at home.

In the early morning I pedaled up to the Umfolozi Game Reserve with all the excitement of a little kid on his first visit to the zoo. The warden in the booth stared at me in disbelief. "You realize I can't let you in on that," he stated.

"I'll pedal really fast," I joked.

He rolled his eyes and shook his head.

Actually, I had just assumed there would be a shuttle bus service or some type of public transportation. Nothing of that sort. My only option was to hitchhike.

I was already at a disadvantage, though. With a fully loaded touring bike, I could only hope to get a ride with someone who had a truck. I had also unwittingly chosen the unpopular southwestern gate. One vehicle every other hour passed by. For eleven hours I stood by the gate, staring into the reserve.

As the sun began to set, the game warden took pity on me. "I'm off duty now and heading in. Throw your bike in the back of the *baakie*."

We proceeded to scream through the park. For the first time in my life I saw giraffes and rhinos and kudus in the wild … all at fifty miles an hour. The excitement of discovery mixed with absolute terror. I hung on for dear life in the back of the truck, trying to keep both me and my gear from bouncing out.

We pulled up to the reserve headquarters in the middle of the park. Minutes later we were back in the truck. The reserve was completely full, most reservations having been made years in advance. The warden could only drive me to the exit on the other side of the reserve.

As he helped me unload my bike he said, "I'll be honest with you. Considering the area we're in, you are probably safer inside the fence with the animals than out here. But rules are rules. Be careful."

My first sojourn into a game reserve had been a complete disaster.

Two days later I cycled up to the entrance of a private reserve. No one was manning the gate. An illustrated sign warned of wild animals and another showed a hungry lion growling at two strolling stick figures. A large red *X* had been painted over the figures—the international symbol for "no walking on the wild side."

What was I to do? The noonday sun beat down with a vengeance and I hadn't spied a vehicle for hours. Backtracking and going around the reserve would take an extra day. Tired and frustrated, I reasoned that since there was no sign prohibiting bicycles, I wouldn't be breaking any rules ... and it was only four kilometers.

Halfway across I encountered a man dressed in khakis and shouldering a rifle. He put up his hand, signaling me to stop. Behind him were two tribal women with baskets balanced on their heads. "Are you not afraid?" he inquired. "Not really," I replied without much conviction.

This man was paid to escort locals along the four-kilometer stretch that connected two public roads. He told me if I wanted to play it safe, I could walk back with him to where I'd begun and then wait for the next official armed crossing. But I was tired of the waiting game. I decided to take my chances and pedaled forward. The escort shook his head slowly in disbelief and walked on, trailed by the two women.

The road was straight and flat, running through open savanna. The surroundings were exactly the same as I'd been riding through for days, but the possibility of lions lurking about got both my heart and my adrenaline pumping. I must admit to picking up my pace and scanning every bush after meeting the armed escort. I reached the other gate without incident. The locals were probably a little paranoid.

Later on that afternoon I met a game ranger while photographing a half-dozen giraffes. He assumed that I had come along the main highway, instead of cutting through the game reserve.

"I'd let you bicycle through the reserve," he said, pointing in the direction of the road I'd just traveled, "but you wouldn't last long."

"Why?" I inquired.

"First. This private reserve has the largest concentration of lions and leopards in South Africa. Second. Riding a bicycle is actually much more dangerous than walking. You see, lions are cats and as you probably know, cats like to chase things. They wouldn't eat you unless they were hungry. They'd just bat you around a bit."

A feeling of nausea swept over me and my knees grew weak as I realized how stupid I'd been. Only fate and good fortune had kept me from becoming the ultimate chewy toy for a seven-hundred-pound cat.

In the following weeks I explored nature reserves in Natal and the Transvaal, but left my bicycle at the gates, hitching rides with other visitors. At Umfolozi Reserve I saw both white and black rhinos, one of the last places on earth where these two species still roam. At Mkuze, hippos snorted and grunted while lounging in a river lined with crocodiles. At Kruger National Park, the largest in South Africa, I watched and listened to a leopard dine on a tortoise, cracking and crunching away. Later that same afternoon I gazed in wonder and then terror as a bull elephant charged up to our vehicle while our driver searched for first gear. Wildebeests, fish eagles, kudus, zebras, jackals … each park brought new sightings and new wonders.

Although I gazed through my binoculars until my eyes ached, never once did I even catch a glimpse of a lion. Considering my lapse of intelligence and reason, I am truly thankful I'm alive to tell you how disappointed I am.

Swaziland Cowboy

I CLOSED MY EYES, HELD MY BREATH, AND DUCKED MY HEAD TO protect my face from flying gravel. The rainless winter had left Swaziland's unpaved roads bone dry. The truck passed at twice the posted speed limit and my world turned brown as huge clouds of dust mushroomed in every direction. I coughed as the fine, gritty powder settled, sticking to every exposed, sweaty part of my body. This scenario was repeated with every passing vehicle, providing me with a temporary tan and a new nickname—"Topsoil Willie."

In spite of these frequent dustings, I was enjoying Swaziland. It had a laid-back, friendly feel to it. Many of the locals wore brightly colored tribal dress as opposed to the Los Angeles Lakers and Chicago Bulls T-shirts and caps that are the rage in South Africa.

My severely parched throat needed something, anything, cool to drink. It was Sunday and many of the small shops were closed so I pulled in to a service station. Once inside, my ears captured a familiar sound, one they had not heard for months. From a small radio in the corner of the snack shop came the unmistakable twangs of a pedal steel guitar.

"Do you like this music?" asked the attendant as he entered the shop. "Radio Swazi plays country-western from one to two o'clock on Sunday afternoons. I never miss it. But my own collection is nothing but Don Williams."

I ran through the limited list of country artists I knew. "Dwight? Kenny? Dolly? Hank?"

"You can have them all. Don's the best."

I ordered a soft drink.

"I want to go to America," the attendant continued, "to Texas and ride a horse. Cowboy life is the best. Do you want to see something?"

Before I could answer, there was a loud "clunk." He had swung his leg up onto the counter, displaying a finely oiled and polished cowboy boot. "Now I can die with my boots on. Just like in the movies. How much for a horse in your country?"

I admitted that I didn't know the going price for a stallion, then asked him his name.

"Bheki."

"Becky?"

"Yes, Bheki."

"Well, Becky. If you ever find yourself deep in the heart of Texas and belly up to a bar, you might consider a name change."

"Why?" he asked, handing me a Pine-Nut soda, which tasted nothing like pines or nuts.

"You may not get the reaction you want when you say, 'Howdy, pardners. My name's Becky.' It just isn't a cowboy name." I avoided bringing up the gender issue.

Bheki swaggered out to the pump to service a police vehicle, his boots not quite matching the yellow-and-red company coveralls. More vehicles pulled in and it became apparent our conversation would not continue. I tried to get his attention, but Bheki was busy adding a quart of oil to a logging truck.

I pulled onto the highway and began coasting down a hill when there came a voice calling, "Hey Willie! My name is Bheki, but you can call me Don!"

I gave him a thumbs-up and we exchanged a final wave. It was sad in a cinematic sort of way. The Swaziland Cowboy stood station-bound and it was I who rode off into the sunset.

Video Night in Venda

LITTLE CHILDREN RAN FROM ME IN TEARS. OLD WOMEN AVOIDED any eye contact and quickly passed by. Young boys stared at me from behind the safety of a row of bushes. What was I doing? Nothing, other than walking into a general store in the former homeland of Venda.

Inside, standing behind the counter, I met Zachariah, a young handsome black man in his twenties. I asked him if they had any pasta or canned soup. He handed me a couple of cans of stew and apologized about the lack of noodles.

I then asked if he would mind explaining the horrified reception I'd just received.

"It is *not* you and it *is* you. You must understand. I cannot remember the last time a white man walked into this store. And considering recent history, the only reason one would be doing so is to bring some very bad news or to arrest someone."

I thanked him for resurrecting my self-esteem, paid for my groceries, and pedaled on.

About a mile down the road I put on the brakes. "Where are you going, Willie? You just left your adventure back at the store." Zachariah spoke perfect English in an area where almost everyone spoke a tribal dialect and/or Afrikaans. I had left my only interpreter back at the store.

When I walked back into the shop after once again terrifying the local youth, Zachariah smiled broadly and asked, "What did you forget?"

"Nothing. Would you mind if I spent the rest of the afternoon with you here at the store?"

His smile grew even wider, "It has been so long since I've practiced my English. I would be delighted."

We sat out on the porch on two rocking chairs. One by one, the little kids approached. Zachariah answered their questions about the white man, and after a couple of hours I was playing trucks with the kids and cards with the men

Afternoon turned into evening. When Vincent, the store owner and a bachelor, arrived in his pickup truck, I was immediately invited to be his guest for the night.

His bachelor pad was nothing more than the storeroom attached to the shop.

The room had no furniture, but was equipped with a stereo, CD player, color TV, and VCR. I found a comfortable place to sit on the floor, with a forty-pound sack of dried Mopane worms to lean back against.

Our dinner consisted of scrambled eggs, baked beans, and mealie pap porridge (cornmeal and water cooked to the consistency of play dough). I had to move for dessert. Vincent dug into the bag and handed out handfuls of the dried Mopane worms.

Zachariah explained they were actually caterpillars of the emperor moth and considered a delicacy in Venda. They are best when freshly harvested and quickly deep-fat fried, so that the outside is crunchy and the middle stays soft. I was happy to take his word for this.

The dried variety, I found, had the consistency of a thick overdone potato chips and tasted a lot like dirt.

The last red hues of sunset faded, so Vincent cranked up the generator. A single, bare sixty-watt bulb, swinging in the middle of the room, pulsed.

A group of nine young men soon arrived, filling the room to capacity. A video was selected from a cardboard box in the corner. I knew my chances of viewing a South African "art" film were anorexically slim. Then up popped Chuck to prove me right (that's Norris, not Heston). I have successfully avoided Mr. Norris's films in the United States, but have been subjected to them in Mexico, Central America, India, and now South Africa. I didn't catch the title, but Chuck seemed intent on destroying half of Vietnam.

Twenty minutes into the movie, Vincent decided to listen to some music, so he turned off the volume of the TV. This warranted no response from the other viewers. Catching the dialogue was not necessary—none of them spoke English, and Chuck breaking necks and machine-gunning battalions translates without the need for subtitles. But I wasn't prepared for what was to come out of the speakers. Dolly Parton. "Nine to Five (What a Way to Make a Livin')." This was now the soundtrack to a Chuck Norris film.

It was one of those travel moments when you check to see if you're awake, because reality couldn't be this bizarre. There I was, sitting in a village in South Africa, munching on dried Mopane worms, watching Chuck blast his way through Vietnam with the vocal support of Dolly while, simultaneously, singing and chanting could be heard from across the road where several boys were going through initiation ceremonies (which I was not allowed to attend).

This comic cultural potpourri was too much for me and I began to giggle. I bit my lip to try and restrain myself, but finally the laughter burst out. Every head turned in the room as if on cue. Every face reflected annoyance or outright anger. I looked up at the television screen only to discover that Chuck Norris was getting the crap beaten out of him. The only interpretation of my actions? I was making a mockery of their hero. I turned to my savior, Zachariah. He'd left the building. I had no way of explaining. I shrugged my shoulders and smiled, while my brain raced. "How do I get out of this one besides bolting for the door?"

In an instant, Chuck disappeared, Dolly was silenced, and we were all pitched into darkness. I was saved. It is the only party in the world I've been to that ran out of gas, literally. Chuck's victory would have to wait for another video night in Venda ... for there was not a drop of kerosene left for the generator.

PJ and Farky

EVERY LONG BICYCLE JOURNEY HAS THEM. THOSE STRETCHES OF scenic sameness that dull the mind and numb the butt. The boring parts. Sections of a nation or continent that most people skip or drive through at seventy miles an hour at night. Across the United States it's the endless cornfields of South Dakota. In Canada the wheat-growing region of Saskatchewan literally stretches on for days in bicycle time. In South Africa it's the bushveldt or "veldt." Hundreds of kilometers of flat roads crossing dry, scrub-filled plains.

Years prior, I might have been tempted to catch the nearest train, but experience has taught me that dull places are most often colored with local characters.

Enter PJ and Farky. A nearly blind, one-armed, one-legged rancher and his pet mongoose. PJ's the one who drives the cattle. Farky's the one partial to ankles and shoelaces.

After eight hours of pedaling through the veldt, I pulled off the road, looking for a place to camp.

PJ met me at the gate. Farky climbed straight up my leg, coming to a stop on my shoulder. His tiny black eyes stared at the rearview mirror attached to my helmet.

"Don't mind him. He's got less than decent manners."

Farky gave my ear a couple of sniffs and climbed down and began gnawing on my shoelaces.

"Looks like you need a shower and a bed. Come on inside."

On the walk up to the house, I learned that PJ had worked as an electrician. One evening, as he was replacing a high-voltage wire, the cable was struck by lightning. He lived through it, but lost his right arm and leg and 80 percent of his vision. His wife left him with their two kids soon after.

"I've only got one arm and one leg to fill up, so there's plenty to eat." He motioned me inside.

Soon I was sitting down to supper with PJ and his eight-year-old son, Peter, and ten-year-old daughter, Elizabeth. Farky had his own chair and place at the table. He gobbled up the food scraps in his small bowl and left to explore under the sofa without asking to be excused. The rest of us took our time with our bread and butter and bowls of mealie pap.

"It hasn't been easy. But what do you do? I had a family to feed, so I found a job running this ranch." Farky emerged from the couch and settled down in PJ's lap.

After dinner, PJ gave me a tour of the ranch.

"Ever try driving a clutch with only half your limbs?"

He threw his crutches in the bed and fired up the old white pick-up. Farky took up his position on the dash. We jerked and swerved down one-lane dirt roads.

"I'm lucky I live out here. No signs to read. No pedestrians to avoid."

PJ would aim the truck straight, give it some gas, switch to the clutch, let go of the steering wheel, and throw it into the next gear, managing to grab the wheel before we landed in the ditch. After my terror subsided, it was fascinating to watch.

Back at the house he showed me to my room.

"I only have one rule in this house. The light stays on in the bathroom and the door stays open. You see, if I come hopping down this hall without my crutch at two in the morning and turn the corner and that door's shut—I'm in trouble." He laughed and winked.

I slept with Farky curled around my head.

In the morning, after breakfast, while I was packing my bike, PJ approached me. "You are welcomed back anytime. I'll probably be dead, but my kids will welcome you." PJ waved good-bye with Farky perched in his callused hand. Calling out. "One more thing. Don't send me a postcard. Send one to your mother instead."

There are times when I feel like I've accomplished great things by pedaling tens of thousand of miles throughout the globe. Then I meet someone like PJ and realize that the true heroes accomplish much greater things with little fanfare and bravado.

Skip over the boring parts? And miss the PJs and Farkys of this world? Never.

Dr. Travel and Mr. Home

"ZIMBABWE—26 KILOMETERS." I LOOKED UP AT THE SIGN AND AN internal struggle began.

I have a split personality like that of Dr. Jekyll and Mr. Hyde. In my life they go under the names of Dr. Travel and Mr. Home.

Dr. Travel loves everything about the road: strange foods, moonlit campsites, dust and sweat, dogeared maps leading to who knows where? The aching muscles, the uncertainty, the challenge. New cultures, new friends, new experiences.

Mr. Home longs for the familiar: lattés at the corner café, baseball games, checking the mailbox. "Where shall we eat? I know where!" The firm mattress, the certainty, the routine. Old favorites, old friends, old times.

Dr. Travel wanted to go on. Forget the expense, follow the baobab trees into "Zim," and cycle clear up to Cairo. What did it matter that he had bookings to speak at schools in the fall? They'd understand. Mr. Home was ready to turn around, to cycle to Johannesburg, and fly back to the States in time for his nephew's birthday. His clothes were wearing thin and his funds were running out.

I sat by the side of the road and ate an apple with some cheese while my two personalities duked it out. By the time I threw the core out into the bushveldt, Mr. Home had won ... this time.

Turning my bicycle around, I began to pedal to Jo'burg.

I reflected on four thousand miles of cycling in South Africa. In my handlebar bag was a book filled with addresses of people I'd met along the way. Folks who had fed me and housed me, given me directions, suggestions, and all but adopted me into their families. South Africa had long ceased to be "that place of apartheid" or "the country often mentioned on CNN." It was now a part of me.

My mind pedaled back across mountains, through villages, and along gravel roads. Back to a town named Clanwilliam in the Cape where I met Theo and Esme in the town park. They shared their picnic lunch with me and also a part of their lives. They were six and eight years old when uniformed men came and informed their families that their neighborhood had been declared a "Whites Only" area. Their families were given three months to move. They talked of anger and shame and of their lifelong struggle for equality.

When we got up to leave Theo said, "You must understand, Willie, five years ago we could not have sat with you in this park. It was for whites only." But this was the "new" South Africa and a white man and a colored man embraced in the park, and for the first time in my life I truly understood the meaning of freedom.

I'm presently on a flight to Los Angeles. Mr. Home is ecstatic and will soon be back to familiar surroundings. Maybe my travel days are numbered. Maybe it's time to settle down. Get a job with stability and a pension plan. Who am I trying to kid? Dr. Travel is gazing at the world map in the in-flight magazine ... planning, dreaming. It's only a matter of time.

The Balkans

Bicycle Route ———
Train Route ·······

May 1996–October 1996

Map Key

"You're insane!" That was probably the most frequent response when I told people I was going to bicycle the Balkans, followed by, "Watch out for mines."

I rarely argued or tried to explain. As soon as people heard "Balkans," they thought "Bosnia." Friends imagined me spending five months dodging bullets and land mines.

It was the region, not the war, that fascinated me. Slovenia with its mountains, Romania with its Gypsies and painted churches, the Black Sea coast, and the rarely explored countries of Macedonia and Albania.

Everything was set. I knew the routine. I would be leaving once again on a four- to five-month solo bicycle journey as I had every year for the past six. My commentary series would once again be heard on public radio station KUOW. I had a new bike provided for me by Rodriguez, new waterproof panniers provided by Ortlieb, and new underwear provided by Mom.

Many people envied my lifestyle—"footloose and fancy free." Through speaking engagements and part-time work I managed to save enough money in seven months to pay for my travels the other five. Not many people get to do what they really love for a living and I was one of them.

But I wasn't happy as the plane lifted off from Seattle's airport bound for Budapest. My heart was not in the adventure ahead. It was back in Seattle, grounded. I had gone and done the one thing a wanderer should never do. I'd fallen in love.

Depressed in Budapest

I LOOKED OUT AT THE RIVER SEINE FROM ONE OF THE BRIDGES that connects the cities Buda and Pest. Cloudy skies cast a dim light on its waters and the busy streets of Hungary's capital.

I was depressed. Professional wanderers aren't supposed to fall in love. This one had.

Four magical months after literally bumping into her at the Highland ice-skating rink, I left the woman whom my little nephew fondly calls "Kissie Girl" behind in Seattle. In the weeks prior to our tearful departure at the airport, I kept telling myself it wouldn't be so hard. I was wrong.

Other factors added to my darkened mood. On arriving in Amsterdam I was told I had "ceased to exist" in the airline's grand computer reservations system, and it might be days before I could fly on to my destination. I spent four hours alternately arguing, demanding, and pleading before I was issued a seat.

At the Budapest Airport my bike box emerged in such a condition that I could only venture two guesses: It had been rolled down several flights of stairs, or the handlers had used it for kick-boxing practice.

Now it was beginning to rain. I reminded myself again that I'd made a wise decision in not asking her to join me. Cycling through Bosnia is not the best way to introduce anyone to bicycle touring.

No sooner had those thoughts flashed through my brain than I heard a bicycle bell and turned to see a young couple on their fully loaded tandem bike waving to me. Although they spoke in a language I didn't understand, I clearly heard, "You idiot. She'll probably meet the man of her dreams while you're fixing a flat in Bulgaria."

The rain turned to drizzle and I pedaled into the business district. I leaned my bike against a McDonald's and took refuge in a phone booth. While the rain turned to heavy showers, I practiced feeling sorry for myself.

I watched as, one by one, umbrellas began to open—yellow, green, red, and blue—each adding a splotch of color to the gray cobblestone street. Laughter wafted into my booth of sorrows as lovers, schoolkids, lawyers, and shoppers dashed for cover. A fat man waddled by wearing a plastic shopping bag as a temporary helmet. A little boy stomped a puddle up onto his father's slacks. By now there were so many umbrellas open that the corner resembled a giant multicolored azalea. The air no longer smelled of diesel exhaust but of spring.

A loud rapping startled me, and I looked out to see a sopping wet gentleman holding a phone card. I couldn't think of anyone to call locally at the moment, so I emerged from my protective shell, running to my bike. While I was frantically digging for my rain jacket, I burst into a jag of spontaneous laughter. I wasn't sure why, but at that moment I was ready for a new adventure.

I pedaled down the rain-soaked boulevard spraying gritty fishtails from my wheels. But only one thought kept a smile on my face. At the end of my journey, I have a date with Kissie Girl. We are scheduled to meet at noon on September 27 at the Parthenon in Greece.

I'll be there. I promise.

Veggie Pizza

I SCANNED DOWN THE FIRST THREE PAGES OF THE MENU OF Restaurant Da Wally in Budapest. It was printed in Magyar, the national language of Hungary, so not a single word did I understand. Rob, my table companion, was having the same problem. We had wandered over from the backpacker's hostel, where the motto appeared to be, "Drink till the bars close, then climb a bridge."

On his summer vacation from a private college in Boston, Rob was not in Eastern Europe to study architecture, visit art galleries, or attend the opera. He was there to meet women. "Have you seen what girls wear here. They would get arrested in the small town I'm from. I don't know about you, but I'm in heaven. But I have to tell you, hope this doesn't bum you out. The women in Prague are twice as hot." I raised my eyebrows and chuckled as if to say, "Really?" when I was actually thinking, "I feel really old at this moment."

Rob was in the midst of an impassioned exposé on how to pick up Hungarian babes when my eyes latched onto a familiar word, *pizza*. Now I could have ordered *fogas* or *kacsa* or even *zsemlt*, but I had no idea whether they were animal or vegetable, raw or cooked, solid or liquid. I wasn't in the mood for cuisine roulette, so I unadventurously ordered a large veggie pizza.

A half an hour later, my meal arrived topped handsomely with yellow and green bits. Handpicked peppers? Summer squash? Chives?

Closer inspection revealed canned corn and canned peas randomly distributed atop lukewarm cheese.

"Whoa. Now that is one gnarly-looking pie," Rob commented. "I'm glad I ordered plain cheese."

I didn't want to attempt to complain in a language I did not speak—and it was a veggie pizza after all. The menu hadn't specified what *kinds* of vegetables … and it was large.

As I was brought up to do so, I ate the whole soggy disc, using both hands to keep peas and corn from rolling onto my lap.

Rob belched as he drained his third beer. "The pizza's better in Prague too. You want to check out a couple of bars?" I graciously passed.

Sixteen hours later, after my digestive system had managed to sort out the whole sordid affair, I was ready to try again.

While wandering a back street, the clatter of plates and flatware drew me into a dreary, hole-in-the-wall establishment. The tiniest of signs read "Bufe." This was where the local workers rubbed elbows—literally. There were no tables, only waist-high counters to dine on. The place was packed, a reassuring sign.

I slipped into the line composed mostly of working-class men in tattered wool coats. The gentleman next to me kindly informed me of the names of the dishes others were eating as I pointed to them while we shuffled forward in line with our trays. Suddenly his face lit up and he said, "Goulash. You like goulash?" "Goulash" was again repeated, but this time from the kitchen. The cook waddled her way up front, smiling. "Goulash. You like?" I nodded yes and her smile widened impossibly farther as she clasped her hands to her chest.

Seconds later I stood in front of a steaming bowl of potatoes in a savory broth with large tender pieces of meat spiced with paprika. Large slabs of brown bread were provided for dunking.

As I ate I occasionally glanced over my shoulder and caught the cook proudly watching. I nodded, toasting her with my spoon, held high.

"Hold the veggie pizza, folks," I thought to myself. "I'm in a goulash state of mind."

Cool Reception

"COLLEAGUE!" (COL-EE-GAY) THE MAN BELLOWED AS HE SLAPPED me on the back and poured me another glass of white wine with a splash of seltzer. I was quickly getting drunk on a humid Sunday afternoon in Dubrovnik, Slovenia, surrounded by men sweating in suits. I would soon need to make a hasty retreat or somehow drastically influence the wine-to-seltzer ratio.

What was the occasion? I had no idea yet. But it beat the fate of hundreds of sweaty truckers only ten miles away. The border of Hungary and Slovenia is closed to commercial vehicles on weekends, so a seemingly endless line-up of trucks had stretched for miles. I counted as I cycled past the big rigs parked on the side of the shadeless highway, losing track at over four hundred before reaching the border. My big rig only weighed eighty pounds, even with the four large sausages and hunks of cheese I'd purchased on the tip that food prices were double in Slovenia, so I had been quickly waved through.

What I didn't realize is the party had only begun. Ludwik motioned me to leave my bike outside and follow him. He opened the door to the local meeting hall. Cool air, laughter, and music spilled out. Several tables were decked with fine linen and piled with meats, cheeses, and elegant desserts. White and pink ribbons hung from the concrete ceiling and draped above the stage.

Ludwik put his arm around my shoulder and announced me as his friend to the bride, the groom, and anyone within earshot, "Colleague." The wedding party now numbered over a hundred well-dressed guests and one dirty, smelly cyclist.

I was served a large platter of what appeared to be the entire spectrum of Hungarian cuisine. The four-piece band, including a electric guitarist, bass player, drummer, and—to round out the mix—a keyboard player with plaid pants, jacket, and vest right out of Sergeant Pepper, picked up the tempo. The pounding polka beat reverberated off the walls and the shiny linoleum floor. I watched as guests of all ages danced and twirled about the room. More wine and even less seltzer. The volume soared as everyone joined in the singing.

Ludwik sat next to me singing and slapping his knee to the beat, breaking his cadence occasionally to slap me on the back and yell, "Colleague!"

Many of the guests had left their seats around the large round tables heaped with food and set up along the perimeter of the hall, and now were dancing arm-in-arm. Ludwik grabbed my elbow with his meaty hand and in one smooth motion lifted me out of my chair.

The two of us joined the dance. I was thrust between two older ladies who appeared to find my placement in the circle inappropriate and sent me down the line twixt two younger, single women.

Ludwik's wife grabbed a hat and a cane adorned with ribbons and danced a solo in the middle of the circle. Where was all this frivolity at the weddings I'd attended in the United States? I pondered as I stumbled through the steps. All I could remember were polite reception lines and tasteless white sponge cake. Yet there I was laughing and whirling about a reception hall in foreign land, dancing with people whose names and language I didn't know.

The feverish dance ended and I was introduced to the bride and groom and the bride's father and mother. (Thank God I was wearing my formal black cycling shorts.)

As Ludwik escorted me outside, I turned and the entire reception party (including the band) stopped what they were doing and waved good-bye in unison. It was right out of *The Sound of Music*.

Ludwik gave me a kiss on each cheek and a huge bear hug. I was back to pedaling again, full of food and wine, with one last "Colleague" ringing in my ears.

Bicycles are magic. They open doors. At least for me they have. To homes, huts, and hovels across the world; to fiestas in Mexico, festivals in India, ceremonies in South Africa, and now a wedding reception in Slovenia.

Would Ludwik have waved me over if I had been waiting at the bus stop or driving a rental car or simply strolling by? I doubt it. But because I'm riding this gear-laden, human-powered, open-air vehicle, I've been in Slovenia for less than four hours and already have a memory to last a lifetime.

You Say Slovakia
I Say Slovenia
(Let's call the whole thing off)

LARGE, DARK THUNDERCLOUDS HAD DEVELOPED AND WERE depositing their contents in the form of heavy rain. This is generally not a problem for me. The panniers on my bike are 100 percent waterproof. You could throw my bike in the river and when you fished it out, my stuff would still be dry. But during this 1 A.M. deluge, I wasn't on my bike—I was in my tent.

My tent is approximately 98 percent waterproof. This 2 percent leakage translated into a lot of water over the course of the storm. After two hours, the inside of my tent qualified as a wetland.

This is the time when, at ten years old and camping with friends in your backyard, you dash inside, your mom makes you hot chocolate, and you watch a bad science fiction movie on TV. At thirty-four, and camping at the base of the Julian Alps in Slovenia, you gather everything to the driest part of the tent and shiver while waiting for sunrise.

It is amazing how slowly five hours can pass while sitting alone in a cold, wet tent. I tried to focus on warm, sunny thoughts, but only managed to dwell on what mistakes I may have made on my tax return and, "Why didn't I learn to play the piano?"

Morning came and brought with it sunny skies and clear, crisp views of the Julian Alps. Compared to my previous night's endeavor, cycling up the steep, winding Vrsic (Ver-seech) Pass was a pleasure. The views were too spectacular to dwell on what parts of my body were aching.

At the top there was a small snack stand and a couple of picnic tables. A short, smartly dressed man in his sixties asked me where I was traveling.

"Through the Balkans," I answered.

"But you're in the Alps, are you not?" came his swift reply.

"Fair enough. I'm cycling Eastern Europe."

I might as well have slapped him in the face.

"Slovenia is not Eastern Europe!" he said tersely. "It is part of the West."

His reaction didn't surprise me. I have observed that Slovenia has an image problem. (Without looking at a current map, could you tell me where it is?) Most people get it confused with Slovakia, and the rest don't even know that it exists. In case you're still pondering, Slovenia (once part of the former Yugoslavia) is the Massachusetts-sized country that borders Austria, Croatia, Hungary, and Italy. Slovenia only saw nine days of war back in 1991, but its tourist industry is still feeling the negative effects.

I showed the man my guidebook, which classified Slovenia as an Eastern European country.

"Your guidebook is wrong."

I tried to explain to him my problem. "You see, I told everyone back home that I was cycling the Balkans, but I began in Hungary, which doesn't qualify. And now you tell me that not only am I not in the Balkans, I'm not even in Eastern Europe."

He leaned over and with a grin said, "Why don't you just tell them you are cycling a piece of the world and leave it at that?" We shook hands and departed without further international incident.

So there you have it. My problem solved, I'll continue to cycle a piece of the world. If I happen to wander into the Balkans and someone agrees to let me call it that, I'll let you know.

Barely Camping

I STARED AT THE BILL IN DISBELIEF. THERE WAS A SITE FEE, A PER-person fee, a national tax, a tourist tax, and a puzzling "first day" tax … all totaling over sixty *kuna* (almost eleven dollars) for a small patch of earth on which to pitch my tent, with an odoriferous toilet nearby. I could get a room at an inn for fifteen dollars. This was ridiculous.

Camping on the highly touristed Croatian Islands in the Gulf of Kvarner was getting on my nerves. Peak season was fast approaching and the campgrounds were filling up. This area, having been far from the front lines of the war, was recovering more quickly than the resorts farther south. This is where Germany comes on holiday, as evident from all prices being first quoted in Deutchmarks rather than in *kuna*, the local currency.

Now I am, without argument, a frugal traveler. That is an understatement. I am the gypsy king of budget travelers—frugal with a capital *FRU*. Tourist boards do not have me in mind when they print their flashy, high-gloss brochures. When given the option, I'd much prefer bunking in a farmer's hayloft (or next to the pig trough, for that matter) than staying in an organized campground. But when no other option is available, it is my opinion that nowhere on earth should it cost one person more than ten dollars to pitch a tent (even if it includes a free round of mini-golf).

I pondered my bill, especially that "first day tax"—what was that? "First day we're going to rip you off?" The way things were going, I either had to hightail it out of Croatia or do something drastic. I decided to take action. I took my clothes off.

You see, Croatia has a series of nudist campgrounds, distinguished by a sign with the letters *FKK* and by the absence of tan lines. They are secluded (for obvious reasons), well maintained, clean, and cost quite a bit less than regular campgrounds. I realized that if I was willing to shed my clothing, I could shed 30 to 40 percent of my camping budget.

While searching for the ferry terminal on the Island of Krk, I happened upon one such establishment. I was a bit reluctant at first, but frugality won out. Besides, this would allow me to live out one of my recurring dreams … bicycling naked.

For those who are curious, not everyone was sans clothing. The receptionist was fully clothed. The maintenance man using the Weed Whacker was too. On the tennis court, there was a sportily dressed man playing against a woman in nothing but Nikes. Disrobing was not a requirement, simply the norm.

After pitching my tent, I decided to leave my clothing behind and walk down to the beach, determined to blend in with the well-oiled, bronzed crowd. My first strides "au naturel" were tentative at best. I was so hyperaware of my body that I couldn't handle the simple mechanics of walking. My arms and legs were out of sync, and the more I concentrated on it, the worse it got. I progressed slowly, looking like a clumsy, traveling tai-chi instructor.

As soon as I had the opportunity, I planted myself near the water's edge and placed my hands on my hips in my best pose of relaxed ambivalence. I wondered why I was getting more than my fair share of gazes, until I realized that while my face, arms, and legs were tan, the rest of my body was a pasty, Seattle-winter white. My chest reflected the afternoon sun with the efficiency of a well-polished mirror, branding me an outsider.

But the novelty soon wore off and I was warmly accepted into the camping community. I played some volleyball, watched a flaming red sunset, and for the first time in my camping career, washed *all* of my clothes ... without having to worry about what to wear while they dried. My only disappointment? Cycling naked is as uncomfortable as it sounds and should be forever relegated to the realm of fantasy.

So I'll leave you with this travel tip: When in need of a campsite while wandering Croatia, look for the "FKK" sign. Not only will you have fewer tan lines, you'll save a few *kuna* as well—even after factoring in the cost of extra sunscreen.

Su and Mosquito

SU LOOKED AT ME AND SAID, "YOU'RE A FREAK, SEATTLE-MAN. I like freaks."

The bushy-bearded, barrel-chested Croatian wearing a long-sleeved peasant shirt raised his glass and toasted me with what, to my taste, appeared to be pure alcohol. Su was his nickname.

"I didn't like your Mr. Clinton at first, but now I am a big fan." He offered me a large chunk of bread and the slab of meat on the end of his military knife.

I owed this meeting to a tiny winding road I spotted from the ferry that sails from the island of Rab to Croatia's coast. My original plan had been to cycle down the shoreline. But the coastal road was also the main highway. And I have discovered that wide roads lead to destinations. Narrow roads lead to adventures. This road had adventure written all over it—steeply snaking and switchbacking its way up into the Velebit Mountains.

It was slow going due to the severe grades and loose gravel. I watched the islands below disappear in the darkness, then reappear in the moonlight. I slept out in the open near the road.

The next morning I reached the top and a hiker's cabin, where I met Su ... and Mosquito.

Mosquito was as thin as Su was round. He wore bright yellow and blue shirts, multicolored pants, and strapped to his enormous backpack was an open, bright blue umbrella.

He had hiked and guided others through the Velebits for as long as he could remember. When the war came, he traded his umbrella for a gun. He led missions in the same mountains to destroy Serbian communication systems. His girlfriend had been his training officer.

"Many times, Seattle-man," Mosquito said, "the Serb soldiers were only meters away, but I hid like a rabbit." He smiled and pantomimed the scenario.

After lunch, we all hiked down the road and some locals invited us to sit in the shade for a drink outside their war-damaged home. Everyone knew Mosquito. The man who dresses like a rainbow.

He grabbed a guitar and strummed a while. Then he played and sang a song he'd written. A "Croatian freedom song," he called it. It told of a man who fled to Italy because of the war and of a conversation he had with the statue of David.

Mosquito and his girlfriend were departing that day to be the first to hike the length of the Velebits since the war ended. "There is evil in the earth now. The Velebits are strewn with mines. But I will always hike these mountains," Mosquito said defiantly.

At that moment I realized my journey in the Velebits was over. My map didn't even show this road existed. I would have to descend the very pass I'd climbed and return to the coastal road.

Su must have seen the disappointment on my face as I turned my bike around. He took a well-worn forest service map out of his pack. "You'll need this or you'll get lost, Seattle-man. I can show you a safe way." He spread the map out on an old large stump, pointing out where I could get water and a good place to camp. "Most of the mines are north and you are going south, but don't stray too far off this road."

I offered to pay him for the map.

"It is my gift to you, Seattle-man, because you are a freak. The world needs more freaks."

I waved good-bye to all three. Mosquito pumped his umbrella up and down in a silly farewell. I pedaled off into the woods, thinking about Su's statement. I took it only as the highest form of compliment.

Bilisane

THE CHURCH OF BILISANE IN THE DISTANCE WAS INVITING. ITS steeple rising far above the trees promised a safe place to camp. On the outskirts of town I passed a car parked on the side of the road. It had no wheels, no windows, and several bullet holes. The first house looked normal, from a distance. Constructed of gray cinder blocks with a red-shingled roof. But long, black, sooty streaks led to broken windows and the remnants of fire. I passed more cars and more homes. The same. Only the church appeared unscathed.

I got off my bicycle and gazed around me. Only that morning, a mere forty kilometers away, I had been laughing with Marco, Mierko, and Sonja at their holiday beach cottage on Croatia's coast. Ten kilometers back I'd cycled through Obrovitz and saw signs of the war—several bombed-out buildings and many others pockmarked from bullets. But there was activity and its people were rebuilding. Where were the people of Bilisane?

I approached the church through high weeds. An open door to a church is usually inviting. This one was daunting.

The smell of bird droppings and plaster dust greeted me as I stepped inside. There were no pews or benches left. A wooden desk sat askew in one corner. Every drawer had been wrenched open and what remained of the contents lay strewn on the floor. Some of the paintings had been ripped or removed from the walls. An iron candelabra hung from the ceiling, its candleholders bent or detached. Only a makeshift lectern, draped in an orange tapestry embroidered with a cross, looked in place, as if someone had returned and gently placed it so.

Bits of broken glass and plaster crunched and popped beneath my feet as I walked about. My heart skipped a beat as I startled a pigeon and it escaped through broken windows.

I stood in the middle of the sanctuary, uneasy and afraid. In the thirty minutes I'd been in Bilisane I had not heard a sound other than crickets and birds. No cars. No dogs barking. No kids playing. It was my ears, not my eyes, that finally pronounced Bilisane dead.

I broke the eerie silence in the only way that seemed appropriate. I sang a couple of verses of a hymn I learned as a child. I'd always loved the way your voice echoes in a church. Now it only made me want to cry. I pitched my tent in the nearby woods and tried to fall asleep, listening to the birds and crickets … and nothing more.

My next day's journey brought more of the same. Kastel Zegarski, Ervenik, and every other town and village were deserted—every house burned and gutted. All this contrasted by green fields sprinkled with red poppies and cherry trees full of fruit.

My water bottles were empty, so I cycled to Kistanje, a larger dot on my map, in search of water. I arrived to find wider streets, larger buildings, and the same destruction. A strange sound caught my attention and I looked down the long boulevard. The image will never leave me. There among gutted buildings, rubble, and glass, an old woman, dressed all in black, was sweeping a section of the sidewalk outside of what I assumed was once her home. I asked if there was water. She indicated there was none and continued her sweeping. Her small section of sidewalk was perfectly clean.

Fortunately, I later ran into some U.N. troops, and they filled my water bottles. They informed me the area I'd come through was heavily mined and hoped I hadn't strayed from the road. The towns and villages had been occupied by ethnic Serbs who fled or were killed during the August Croatian offensive.

The people of Bilisane would not be returning. Others would eventually move there, and another town would rise in its place. Bilisane had ceased to exist. It would only be remembered in the hearts of those who had lived there and forever etched in the memory of a weary cyclist who stopped for the night.

Sleeping with the Enemy

CLAD ONLY IN MY CYCLING SHORTS, I STOOD HUNCHED OVER soaping up my hair. Five feet away an old woman with a garden hose waited for her cue. I motioned and she sprayed the icy water. Her target was my head, but her aim being far from perfect, she first hit my leg, then my shoulder. This caused me to squeal, her to laugh, and our audience to howl. Soon I was completely drenched.

Our audience consisted of three families all living together in a small house off the highway between Mostar and Sarajevo. It is a beautiful road, winding through river canyons. But there are no hotels or campgrounds. All have been abandoned or demolished. IFOR tanks and supply trucks outnumber civilian vehicles, and you must slowly cross temporary one-lane pontoon bridges erected next to the twisted wreckage of bridges destroyed.

I had managed to explain my situation in sign language to two men working in a vegetable garden. They gave me permission to set up my tent near their home. I had almost completed the task when a woman came running over yelling and waving her arms. The same woman who now held the hose. She pointed at the tent and I made the assumption I'd soon be departing.

But her anger turned toward the two men. She helped me pack up my tent, not to send me on my way, but to invite me as a guest inside their home. One of the sons helped carry my bike up the stairs and gave up his bed so the traveler could have one.

I winced as another shot from the hose hit me in the chest. I wagged my finger at the old woman, accusing her of having better aim than she claimed. She laughed.

It was inconceivable to me that the family I had eaten lunch with that afternoon—whose children I'd juggled for—wish this woman were dead. She and her family are Muslims. They are Croats.

The house the Croatian family lives in once belonged to Muslims, who fled when the Croat troops shelled Mostar. The house the woman with the hose lives in once belonged to a Croatian family, who fled when Muslim troops retaliated.

Wouldn't it be ironic, I thought, if the two families I'd spent time with that day were unknowingly living in each other's homes.

As a foreigner and a traveler, I am able to pass back and forth between the two (or three) camps without being threatened or asked to take sides. In each I hear stories of the other: I play soccer with a boy whose father was killed by a Serbian mine. I drink a beer with a man whose girlfriend was killed by a Muslim sniper. I talk with a family whose daughter was raped and killed by Croat troops. I'm surrounded by the effects and destruction of war, but I treat the stories as a strange sort of science fiction, because I don't want to believe they're true.

The peace is holding on, but so is the hatred.

I toweled off after hosing down, trying to get all the soap out of my ears. I drank Turkish coffee and showed the three families photos of my own. I gave and was given several hugs good-night.

Then I did what I've done every night since I entered Bosnia. I slept with the enemy.

Border Games

I WAS ON A STRICT TIME SCHEDULE TO GET BACK TO BUDAPEST, and the bridge at Bosanska Gradiska in Bosnia—which spans the Sava River to Croatia—was my shortcut. Denying my right to cross were two Serb policemen. Presenting my case were a Polish U.N. police officer and an interpreter from Belgrade.

I listened without comprehension as they argued back and forth, already anticipating the outcome. The Serbs had guns; my advocates did not. My hunch was right and the interpreter turned and apologized. I would not be allowed to cross.

One hundred and twenty kilometers back I had tried to avoid this scenario, asking a British information officer if I could cross the border at Bosanska Gradiska. Everyone in the office agreed it would not be a problem.

What I hadn't known then was how little the U.N. troops communicated with one another. The French were in Sarajevo, the Americans in Tusla, the Canadians in Bihac, and the Hungarians north of Banja Luka. I had seen more of Bosnia on my bicycle than most of the troops, who were confined to their sectors, had seen.

Back at the border there was talk of trying to smuggle me across in a troop vehicle. "We could approach the Hungarians or the Brits and attempt to smuggle you across in a troop truck," they said, "but it might take a couple of days." I thanked my U.N. team for their efforts and told them I was only a touring cyclist and did not want to be the cause of an international incident.

I turned my bike around and began the backtrack. In a car a 240-kilometer detour is an inconvenience measured in hours. On a loaded mountain bike it is a morale destroyer measured in days.

I pedaled from early morning till dark for three days—sleeping in a field, at a British military camp, and on the couch of a Muslim family. I exited Bosnia via Bihac. Then it was on to Zagreb, where I caught the 1 A.M. express train into Budapest.

Why the rush? She had called and given me the news. There would be no meeting in Greece as promised. My girlfriend, Kat, would not be waiting for me at the Parthenon.

Instead she had accepted my revised invitation, delivered passionately five weeks prior from a phone booth on the border of Italy and Croatia. She had spontaneously agreed to quit her job, put her possessions in storage, and meet me in Budapest. An inexperienced cyclist, Kat would soon be arriving with my refitted old mountain bike, loaded down with her own doubts and fears, to become my travel companion.

Wonderful, exciting, and horrifying news.

A solo traveler for seven years, can I manage being part of a duet? Can she deal with my odd travel habits, accumulated over thirty thousand miles? Can our relationship survive the back roads of Romania? Only time and distance will tell, but it is we, not I, who will cycle on from Budapest.

Midsummer Night's Dream

THERE WAS SOMETHING ABOUT HER SMILE WHEN I MET HER AT the airport. Kat had never been on an overnight bike trip in her life, but she radiated confidence and excitement. The large cardboard box she carried contained my old mountain bike (she didn't have one of her own). The bicycle was scratched and road-weary, having survived over a decade of hard touring. I'd left it behind because I didn't believe it could hold up for another journey. It would *have* to now.

With such brief notice, Kat's training schedule had consisted of riding the bike to work a couple of times. Her bike wobbled under the unfamiliar weight of loaded panniers as we pedaled toward downtown Budapest.

We spent a week in Budapest, thirty-something lovers, walking and cycling through the narrow neighborhood streets and back alleys. We explored museums, saw *La Bohème* at the opera house, and searched for authentic goulash in dark, neighborhood eateries.

I asked Kat to marry me as we gazed across the Danube at the grand parliament building. She said yes.

Neither of us wanted to admit we were apprehensive to finally hit the road. But Budapest was hard on our budget. We said good-bye to Solomon and Elizabeth, the couple who had rented us a room in their flat. The real adventure could now begin.

We pedaled out of the city in the early morning, surrounded by commuter traffic, but by early afternoon we had emerged into the green, sunflower fields of Hungary. As evening approached, Kat inquired where we would sleep. I told her we were in farm country, so we would simply pull over and ask someone if we could pitch our tent on their property. I added that she shouldn't be surprised if we were invited in for dinner.

The pressure was on. I had regaled Kat with stories of the road: tales of India, South Africa, and Central America. Of being invited into people's homes and huts. Of experiencing the world with all of your senses—to not only see a country, but to hear and smell it as well. All of this through the magic of bicycle travel. What if the magic wasn't there for her?

My first inquiry was met with a shaking head and the words "no camping." I shrugged and shot a sheepish grin to Kat. No problem. We'd try another farmhouse. But with each hand-gestured request to camp came the same negative reply. I'd struck out.

We finally found a flat but soggy patch of ground on the edge of a cornfield where we couldn't be seen from the road and set up our tent. We heated up our packaged soup mix as night fell and the mosquitoes swarmed.

I had forgotten how many nights were spent exactly like this on my travels. A journey was not an endless string of cultural pearls. The magic was surrounded by the ordinary, the boring, and the tiresome.

More of the hard realities of cycle touring surfaced in the morning. There had been no water for bathing and we emerged from our tent sore and filthy. Back on the road Kat experienced the unimaginable pain a bicycle seat can inflict on beginners. I saw the look on her face when she first sat down on the bike and asked her to describe what it felt like.

"If it hurt any worse, I'd throw up."

Thirty miles later we pulled into the small village of Hajdúdorog. As we attempted to look through the large keyhole of a Greek Catholic church, the groundskeeper spied us and unlocked the sanctuary.

As we gazed up at the Byzantine-style frescoes painted on the walls and ceiling, he went on and on about a concert. The only thing that we understood for sure, since our Hungarian was limited to two-word phrases entirely related to food, was the big event would be that very evening.

Was it to be a local children's choir? The history of Hungary as interpreted by a mime troop? Traveling Scottish bagpipers? We had no idea, but we decided to take a chance and waited for evening while drinking abysmally bitter cups of coffee in the local sweet shop.

We changed into our formal attire in the city park. ("Formal attire" for a traveling cyclist translates into a clean, wrinkled T-shirt, and sandals worn *with* socks.)

Father Ernest relieved our anxiety about being underdressed when he greeted us wearing a long black cassock that draped down to bright white sneakers.

The group of men who filed into the church were members of "Coro Monte Pasubio," an award-winning choral group visiting from Italy. We were treated to an hour of the finest singing I have ever heard. The audience clapped enthusiastically for encore after encore.

Having secured our bicycles in the church's schoolhouse, we wandered into a restaurant after the concert. In a back room seated at an enormously long table were the members of the chorus and their local supporters. Several people waved us in and we entered to smiles and applause. News of our bicycle journey had spread.

We sat down to glasses of red wine and seltzer. Franco, one of the members who spoke English, acted as our interpreter as we answered questions about our trip and listened to more songs.

At one point we let slip that we were engaged. We hadn't even told our parents yet. But somehow it seemed appropriate to divulge our secret to this man with the voice of an angel.

Two of the last to leave, we exited the restaurant only to find the entire chorus gathered in a semicircle facing us. Franco smiled and said. "It's your fault. You told me you were engaged. Now we Italians, being romantics, must sing for you."

The basses, baritones, and tenors all found their notes, then broke out in laughter after a phrase, discovering they had begun in the wrong key.

The second attempt produced a flawless presentation of the French ballad "Les Plaisirs" (The Pleasures).

Some smiled at us as they sang, others simply closed their eyes. Their voices filled the still night with such sweet harmony it sent chills up and down my spine. I squeezed Kat's hand and we exchanged glances and smiles. Was this real? It had all of the elements of a dream.

We were touched, awed, and somewhat embarrassed all at the same time. Each of the members came up to us afterward and wished us a safe journey and much happiness. The leader gave us one of the group's cassette tapes, and his comments brought a chorus of laughter.

Franco translated, "He says you must listen to this tape before or after "les plaisirs" ... it is a collection of our church songs after all."

Then they all left, on their way to Debrecen and their next engagement, leaving us to bask in the glow of our own personal midsummer night's dream.

The Weight
of Human Kindness

THE BAGS WERE ENORMOUS. THEIR CONTENTS: PEPPERS, cucumbers, containers of yogurt, bread, sandwiches wrapped in tinfoil, potato chips, cookies, a huge bag of cherries, and to top it off, two liter bottles of soda.

It was too much. We couldn't possibly fit it all in our panniers. But we had to. We hadn't been on some insane shopping spree. These were gifts from a Hungarian family who had invited us into their home. Whose fire we'd sat around the night before roasting pork fat. Whose comfortable bed we'd slept in. We hadn't the heart or the vocabulary to refuse one item.

Before we could make our escape, their neighbor added a U.S. military "ready-to-eat" beef stew meal wrapped in heavy brown plastic, and the daughter presented Kat with a stuffed animal. "Sure. Why not? Stuff it in between the sausages another family gave us last week."

At least we would soon enter Romania, where food was scarce, travel guides had warned us. "Expect only bread and dusty bottles of pickled beets on store shelves," one stated. "Stock up on dried soup mixes," added another.

Little did we know that across the border the hospitality would get heavier. That we would purchase one jar of honey and receive two more as gifts. That each time we were invited to stay with locals, we'd leave loaded down with the weight of human kindness. Our heaviest postbreakfast haul? Eight cucumbers, a large glass bottle of hundred-proof homemade plum liquor, and a huge slab of pork fat.

Weight is a serious issue for touring cyclists. It's not like over-packing your four-by-four. Each extra pound teams up with the law of gravity to make life miserable, especially when climbing mountain passes. I've been known to read a novel, cutting out and discarding chapters as I go. But when you stuff twenty pounds of edible gifts in your packs, the fact that you've cut part of the handle off your toothbrush to conserve weight becomes laughably insignificant.

One solution is to toss what we don't need. But we're talking gifts here. You can't throw away gifts! What about redistributing them to others? Easier said than done. I attempted to offer a group of teenagers our unwanted bottles of soda. They thought I was trying to sell them and walked away.

One family gave me an old Swiss army knife. I already had one, so a few days later when it came time to say good-bye to yet another hospitable family, I presented it to the son. My weight-reduction celebration lasted less than a minute as he returned with a gift for me … a larger, heavier knife. It is still sitting at the bottom of one of my packs, for fear that if I give it away I'll get a full cutlery set in return.

Of course, we could always refuse the gifts initially and be known throughout Eastern Europe as "those ungrateful Americans." After much debate and discussion, we have agreed upon a solution that allows us to continue our journey without offending anyone. We've applied for heavy-vehicle permits.

The Thief

WEIGHING IN AT SLIGHTLY UNDER SEVEN POUNDS, IT WAS THE MOST beautiful loaf of bread we had ever seen; a dense, round loaf with a thick golden brown crust, the prize of an entire morning's labor.

Buying a loaf of bread is usually not an adventure. You'd think it would be as simple as cycling along until we spotted a bakery, but this was northern Romania and the small villages we were pedaling through attract little tourist traffic. Why go to all the trouble of putting up a sign when everyone in town already knows where the bakery is?

We located the word for bread in our phrase book—spelled *p-i-i-n-e* with one of those upside-down *v*'s over the first *i*—but we were perplexed on how to pronounce it. With our first attempt an old woman's eyes lit up and she gave directions that led us three kilometers out of town to the river. We still haven't figured out what she thought we asked.

Back in town, our stomachs grumbling, we located a woman carrying a fresh loaf of bread. We chose to use the indication method. We cycled up, smiling broadly while pointing at her loaf, figuring she would show us to the bakery. She, instead, understood that we wanted *her* bread. She scowled, clutched the loaf to her breast, and scooted away. Just as we were about to give up and drink our jar of honey, a woman on her way to church understood our plight and directed us to the "Bruteria." It was there we found our prize.

Taking turns holding the steaming loaf up to our noses, we fantasized about cutting the whole thing in half, slathering it with butter and honey, and eating it on the spot. There was a problem, though. No butter.

Hungry as we were, we decided to search for the missing ingredient. The monster loaf was so large, we couldn't cram it into any of our packs. We settled on bungee-cording it to the back rack of my bike, nestled between my sleeping bag and tent.

We managed to find a small shop (called a "magazine" in Romania) where the owner proudly directed us to a large slab of newly delivered butter. When he discovered we were from America, he insisted we stay for coffee. We hesitated.

From inside the store we wouldn't be able to see our bikes. Normally in a village as small as this one we wouldn't think of being so cautious, but this was Romania and we had been warned about Gypsy thieves a thousand times. The owner saw our concern and posted a little boy outside to guard the bikes.

While we sipped our coffee, made with the hottest tap water available, some local men stopped in for their early-morning shot of brandy. They too warned us repeatedly to watch out for Gypsies— they'd steal our bikes if we left them unattended even for a few seconds. These warnings came with full pantomime, acted out for us in the cramped shop.

The ice cream man then made his scheduled stop. Brandy and chocolate ice cream bars—a winning combination. As we licked and slurped, we opened our maps to show everyone in the magazine our route. But they were much more interested in showing us where we were now and where each of them had been born. We all sat or leaned around a table with our noses buried in a map of Eastern Europe. Thick fingers searched for obscure villages. Suddenly the boy burst in the door, his eyes wide with terror.

I knew in one half of one second that our bikes were gone. While being warned of the Gypsies, we had lost everything to them.

We ran out, hearts pounding. There were our bikes exactly where we had parked them. Why was the boy so upset?

Two bungee cords lay limp. The bread! As precious as it was to us, how fortunate we thought, to learn our lesson and lose so little.

Then we looked across the street. The men standing next to us began to laugh. They laughed so hard they doubled over. The little boy, who seconds before had tears welling in his eyes, giggled uncontrollably. We laughed too, but with an edge of embarrassment. We had jumped so quickly to the stereotypical conclusion. Staring at us was not a band of Gypsy thieves, but a local dairy cow, contentedly chewing our prized loaf of bread.

Sick and Tired

"OH, MY GOD!" I WAS AROUSED FROM A DEEP SLEEP, COCOONED in a down comforter. Kat was sitting straight up in the bed assigned to us by our hosts, a young couple with a newborn who had rescued us as we attempted to pitch our tent in a windstorm at the edge of a cornfield. They had walked us to their nearby farmhouse, fed us, and, because Kat wasn't feeling well, had insisted we sleep in their bed while they slept on the floor in the living room.

The panicked look in Kat's eyes I knew from my own personal experience only too well. She needed a bathroom and she needed one now. But our hosts' cottage lacked plumbing or running water. Kat's refuge lay outside across the courtyard.

She bolted for the bedroom door, flung it open, stumbling over our snoozing hosts on her way to the front door. I then heard her pounding. The door was locked. The husband, in a sleepwalking stupor, located the key and opened the door. Kat sprinted for the outhouse through a cold downpour.

I located my shoes, grabbed an umbrella, and ran out past the pigpen to the small wooden structure. Unexpectedly, I heard laughter from inside. "Are you okay in there?" I inquired.

"Considering I'm in the middle of Romania, sick as a dog, sitting in a foul-smelling outhouse, about to wipe my ass with some kid's old math homework, I guess I'm doing all right." A deep groan preceded another wave of laughter. "We've got to get to a doctor."

Sometimes the fear of going to a doctor in a foreign country can outweigh your need for one. Kat had held out at long as she could. Lots of fluids and positive thoughts just weren't cutting it. But the problem remained, how to find a good doctor? And, preferably, one who spoke English.

In the morning, our hosts, who spoke not a word of English, showed us on the map where we could find medical help. The city of Suceava was about sixty kilometers away. We pedaled for hours in a cold rain, arriving by noon. A gray factory loomed in the distance. As we approached a bridge, I heard a crash and a sharp cry behind me. Kat had fallen. Her wheels had skidded out from under her as she tried to avoid a pothole.

She got up (leaving her bike in the street), walked to the side of the road, knelt down, and burst into tears. She was covered with mud and road grit. I held her as her body shook from both sobs and laughter. "This is too much," she said. "Please tell me this will end soon."

It was only then that I remembered our visit to the small town of Sucevita. There we had briefly met a doctor who had made the journey to the monastery to have his car blessed. He had been in two accidents in two months and thought it was time for some divine intervention.

We had watched as the orthodox priest with his long black robe and long gray beard chanted rapidly, then sprinkled holy water on the dash, the tires, the engine, and finally, in the trunk.

I dug through my wallet, found his card, and studied our rain-soaked map. His clinic was in a village only four kilometers away. After directions from a gas station attendant we soon found ourselves in his waiting room.

The doctor, Stephen, was so excited and surprised to see us that he left several patients waiting while he escorted us upstairs to his private study. His gentle manner and soothing voice quickly put us at ease. We washed up and Katrina, Stephen's wife, brought us something to drink. I was served their finest vodka, while Kat, being sick, was served artificial, neon orange soda.

Kat gave me a longing look of envy, proving she was already on the road to recovery.

After Stephen had attended to his other patients, he came up and greeted us again with a warm hug. We thought we would be in and out in fifteen minutes. But before, during, and after his diagnosis, our doctor and his wife wanted to know everything about our trip, our country, and our families. They set up a small table and we all dined on pork chops and soup. More vodka and orange soda. Our doctor's "visit" spanned six hours and two meals. It was more like a Sunday brunch with questions of "duration of cramps" and "color of stool" thrown in.

We left late in the evening, Kat already feeling well enough to want to pedal. We weren't sure whether it was the medicine or the hospitality that had worked its wonders. It didn't really matter. As we pedaled down the road, Kat, with color back in her cheeks and her dimples once again making my heart do somersaults, summed up the day:

"Where else but Romania could you leave a doctor's office carrying prescription drugs … and a doggy bag?"

No Forwarding Address

THE BURLY, BEARDED MAN AT THE MARKET MOVED QUICKLY FROM behind his produce stand and intercepted me. Our loaded bikes announced "foreign travelers" and he was curious. But it wasn't until I told him where we were from that his excitement rose to a feverish pitch. His eyes grew wide as he announced to the gathering crowd, "America," grabbing me around the shoulders in a one-armed bear hug.

His Romanian I didn't understand, but I interpreted his animated gestures. His fat thumb and clenched fist went up toward his open mouth—there would be drinks. His belly shook—there would be dancing at the local disco. He made a grand gesture toward his stall, promising all of the tomatoes I could carry. Then he made a writing motion on the palm of his hand. All of these things offered in exchange for my address, for a contact in the land of the dollar, a dreamland seen weekly (with subtitles) on Romanian TV in the sunny beaches and perfect tanned bodies of *Baywatch*, and around the clock in music videos, movies, and advertisements. Every third T-shirt in Romania is emblazoned with "America" or "U.S.A."—the land where everybody is rich and drives an expensive car, when not lounging poolside while making business deals with a cellular phone.

One man literally kissed the postcard of Seattle we gave him. He and his wife had won the lottery for two of the limited number of work visas to Canada. But their dream was shattered when they could not raise the three-thousand-dollar fee per person the Romanian government required.

We had cycled through dozens of postcard-worthy villages and towns in Romania. Towns devoid of youth for lack of jobs. It was rare to see anybody between the ages of eighteen and thirty-five. Most were off to the big city of Bucharest to try their luck there. Every young person I talked to would emigrate if given the opportunity. Without travel restrictions and the visa lottery, the country would be empty overnight.

Once confined by Ceausescu and the Communist government, Romanians are now imprisoned by their country's poor economic state. It is rare for the average Romanian to be granted a visa to travel to neighboring countries in Europe, let alone the United States. Here you quickly learn that international travel is not a right, but a granted privilege shared by few.

A contact, a postal address or phone number in America can bring the impossible dream one step closer.

To some I gladly give my address, and truly hope to see them one day in Seattle. But I must be discreet because I cannot afford to house the masses. So, although the burly man persisted, I declined his offers, finally turning my back to him. And yes, it felt cold, callous, and unfair. But the reality is, as an American, I am free to venture off toward Greece, while he is left to dream from behind a mound of rotting tomatoes.

Grandma and Grandpa Bunea

WE STARED UP AT THE VIVID FRESCOES ON THE WALLS AND CEILINGS dating back over three hundred years. The colors leapt out through centuries' worth of accumulated soot. The outside walls were painted as well: scenes of judgment, resurrection, and martyrdom. Adam and Eve, Cain and Abel, Moses.

Kat and I took turns wandering around the monasteries at Voronet, Humor, Putna, and Moldavita while the other kept watch over our bikes. We strolled with other tourists armed with cameras to capture the experience and pockets full of postcards to mail it home to friends and family.

We had read about the painted churches of Bukovina in our guidebooks. "Not to be missed" was the consensus.

But there was something missing for us. We couldn't manage to put a finger on it, but we were disappointed. We both kept waiting for the moment when the experience would overwhelm us and send chills up and down our spines. But the only chills came from the cold breeze penetrating our sweaty T-shirts.

The missing elements wouldn't surface for over a week and several hundred kilometers.

We cycled into the small village of Noul Roman along a dirt track in the late afternoon. The Carpathian Mountains loomed in the distance, our next day's destination. We had managed to snake our way through the back roads without a detailed map by asking locals each time we got to a fork in the road. In the middle of Noul Roman, the road split again.

We had just passed two friendly-looking gentlemen sitting on a bench with their backs resting on the plastered wall of a modest home. They had smiled and waved as we passed. Kat waited at the crossing and I backtracked to ask directions.

The man who we would soon refer to as "Mr. Bunea" indicated that we should take the road that veered right, then he motioned me to follow him into the courtyard of his home. With a grand wave he motioned for Kat to join us.

He was a strong, handsome-looking man, with shocking white hair, dressed in wool pants, a white shirt worn beneath a gray vest, and sporting a matching gray cap. He spoke no English, but his smile beamed a welcome and his laugh charmed.

We sat down to what we thought would be a brief drink. We would not depart for two days.

As we drank the cool well water, his wife, Marie, appeared and discovered two strangers sitting at her garden table. There was not an instant's hesitation—she threw her arms up and welcomed us to their home with a warm hug.

Mr. Bunea indicated that it was getting late and we should not camp but stay in their home. We removed our gear from our bikes and were ushered into their guest room. The old black-and-white photos on the wall revealed that this had probably been their son's room.

After we had changed, Mr. Bunea took us on a tour of their orchard filled with apple trees and a garden brimming with lettuce. Their barn housed a couple of enormous pigs, several chickens, and stalls for two cows. Then he took us down into their cellar and proudly showed off their supply of homemade wine and plum brandy.

The sizzle and smell of pork fat greeted us as we sat back down at the garden table. Maria was busy cooking supper. Although seventy and permanently hunched over from osteoporosis, she was still a fireplug of energy. Her appearance reminded me of a cute apple doll you buy at the fair. But, we would soon learn, an apple doll that could knock back a shot of plum brandy like a sailor.

Later that evening after the cows came home, literally, the Buneas invited over some friends for supper. They spoke English, so we were able to translate stories of our adventure to the Buneas.

We told them of our experience in the painted churches in Bucovina. They asked if we had ever been to an Orthodox service. We explained that we would have liked to, but we were worried that we would offend if we showed up in our cycling clothes.

We learned that the Buneas had been childhood sweethearts and that Mr. Bunea had been the unofficial leader of the village during the brutal reign of Nicolae Ceausescu. Mr. Bunea leaned over and told us, "Years ago if you had stopped and stayed with us, the next morning we would have been taken, blindfolded, to be interrogated."

With no worries of visits from secret police, we laughed and joked the night away, drinking wine and plum brandy. Each time Mr. Bunea raised his glass he bellowed, "William. Katy. *Senetate*" (Romanian for good health).

We awoke the next morning to the sound of cows making their way out to pasture down the main street and to the smell of eggs and pork fat cooking. Mr. Bunea led us to the bathroom where he had stoked the water heater with corncobs so Kat and I could bathe.

It was Sunday and our newfound grandparents had made it clear that we would be attending church with them.

Kat and I searched our packs for our cleanest clothes. But several weeks on the road had left us with only worn and torn alternatives. I tried to imagine in what situation I would feel more self-conscious than in attending a Romanian Orthodox church in cycling shorts and a faded and wrinkled T-shirt.

After breakfast and a hot shower, Maria took us both by the hand and led us upstairs to the attic. There she opened up a grand trunk and began pulling out beautiful black and white garments, embroidered with yellow thread. By the time she was finished, Kat and I were dressed from head to toe in traditional Romanian costumes.

My ensemble fit beautifully, except for the thick leather waist belt that threatened to fall off. Mr. Bunea produced an awl and punched an extra hole for the skinny cyclist. He indicated by patting his belly that if only I'd stick around and eat more of Maria's cooking, the belt would soon fit with no alterations.

We arrived late to the small, freshly painted church and squeezed our way in among about 120 villagers.

The smell of frankincense wafted over us as it had at the monasteries. But here it mixed with the sweat and perfume and body heat of the villagers around us, instead of damp, cold air.

The priest and deacons chanted the liturgy that has barely changed in over a thousand years. Their voices mixed with whispers of "Americans" and "*bicycletas*" and the clinking of coins dropped in silver offering plates.

This is what had been missing from the churches of Bukovina. Life.

Mr. Bunea and I found stiff wooden pews on one side of the church; Kat and Maria stood on the other before being offered seats.

Throughout the service I tried to appear reverent, but I was like a little kid, grinning widely and gazing at everything about me: the candles, the tapestries, the newly painted frescoes, the little boy sneaking bites of a piece of bread, the rough worker's hands that lay formally folded. Occasionally I would catch Kat's eye and we would exchange a "can-you-believe-we're-here?" smile.

After the final "Amens," we filed out of the church and accepted the traditional gifts of bread and luminaries. We stood out in the hot summer sun, but minutes later were ushered back in.

Twin baby boys were being baptized and their mother wanted us to witness it. As the priest sprinkled water on the two squirming babies, Maria grabbed Kat's hand and Mr. Bunea put his hand on my shoulder.

That afternoon we cycled out of Noul Roman—a small village not found in any guidebook. We turned one last time to wave to Mr. Bunea and Maria, our newfound grandparents. And we heard Mr. Bunea's voice as it bellowed. "William. Katy. *Senetate*!"

A Romanian poet once wrote, "Eternity is found in the village."

So is Romania.

Back to School

I ALWAYS HATED THE FIRST DAY OF SCHOOL WHEN I WAS A KID. The transition to first grade was the worst. I was petrified of "not knowing." Not knowing if I would fit in or if my *Yellow Submarine* lunch box would be considered cool or dorky. Not knowing where I would sit or who would talk to me. I wanted to be back in the familiar surroundings of Mrs. Hathaway's kindergarten class.

But after a few days (and a new lunch box), first grade was ever-so-much cooler than kindergarten and I relaxed into my second-row seat behind my new friend, Jorgen.

That same fear visited me when we crossed the border from Romania to Bulgaria. I crossed from a country where after a month of cycling, I felt very comfortable, to a country as daunting as Mrs. Burger's first-grade classroom.

In Bulgaria, I was demoted to the "slow learners" group. I didn't know my numbers. I didn't know how to ask for bread or properly say "hello." (I thought I knew how to say "thank you," but blank stares of incomprehension were the only response I got.) Hell, I didn't even know how to read, as Bulgarian is written in Cyrillic script. It was back to phonics lessons.

Bulgaria was hot, brown, and dirty. I saw fields of dying sunflowers, trash on the side of the road, homes without flower gardens. Little kids and old women peered suspiciously from behind doors.

The August heat beat down and reflected off the pavement and the Communist-era concrete-block apartment buildings.

I wanted to be back in the green hills of Transylvania where I knew how to ask for directions and order coffee (with milk). Where I knew my numbers well enough to haggle the price if need be, and where I could at least pronounce the road signs.

Then yesterday, after my twenty-third attempt at saying "thank you" in Bulgarian, the merchant grinned, almost smiled, as he handed back my change, and a family waved when I said "good day." I had been understood.

Soon thereafter I began to notice the beautiful groves of oak trees in between the brown fields. I enjoyed the unique sound the wooden cart wheels made as they wobbled down the rutted pavement. Looks of suspicion I now viewed as curiosity, and flowers appeared where none had been before.

Just as in first grade, reality hadn't changed, only the way I looked at it. A lesson learned and relearned on the road.

Today it is back to school. We are learning how to count. Our teachers are a group of Bulgarian schoolkids who laugh with us at our mistakes. Today we will learn to count to ten, and Bulgaria will be a cooler, greener, more friendly country for it.

Muxi

"THAT ROAD IS IMPOSSIBLE," THE OLD MAN HAD WARNED US, tapping his index finger on our map as scores of tourists shuffled by on the pedestrian mall. We didn't laugh in his face. We waited until he was out of sight. Impossible? The road we planned to cycle in southern Bulgaria crossed less-than-ominous roads and was clearly marked as paved on our map. He obviously had not grown up in the age of high-tech mountain bikes.

If we had only taken the time and minimal effort to ask him why the road was impossible, he might have mentioned … the flies—*muxi* (moo-hi) in Bulgarian.

As we cycled inland from the Black Sea coast and into the oak forests, they descended upon us—not a couple, not dozens, but swarms in biblical-plague proportions. About half the size of a common house-fly, they circled our heads in thick, black-pepper clouds, seeking out ears, mouths, tear ducts, and nostrils. They seemed to be attracted to two things—movement and sweat. Cycling up the mountain grades, we were the perfect movable feast. But we dined as well, inhaling some and choking on a few more.

We finally resorted to covering our faces with bandannas, leaving only slits to see through. This solved all but the worst of our problems … the constant buzzing. Not the whine of gnats or the low drone of bees; it was more like a chorus of baritone mosquitoes singing an opera from hell.

Our only relief came when we pedaled downhill, as the flies' top speed was fourteen kilometers per hour. But the descents were short lived and at the bottom we needed only to count, "One, two" ... excuse me, these were Bulgarian flies ... "edno, dvei, tri," and they were back. Buzzing. Buzzing. Buzzing.

To avoid going mad, I attempted to enter a Zen-like state. To become one with the flies. To will my body not to sweat. I repeatedly sang a ditty from my childhood as a mantra:

> *Shoo fly don't bother me.*
> Muxi *don't bother me.*
> *Shoo fly don't bother me,*
> *for I'm in love with somebody.*

But then I recalled stories of animals driven over cliffs by hordes of flies. Would this buzzing ever stop? Was it possible we'd have to endure this till Albania? Unable to contain myself any longer, I went into a frenzied swatting session, attempting to kill them all, which sent my bike swerving. Still the buzzing continued, hour after hour.

I have always preferred traveling by bicycle because it allows you to experience a country with all of your senses. In a car, the scenery often passes by like a video on fast forward. But now I envied those who passed in cars, driving through the beautiful oak forests in air-conditioned comfort, while listening to the soundtrack of their choice.

We stopped in a small village and talked with a forester there. He said the flies were so bad, he had to wear goggles when working in the woods. Hoping for some encouraging news, we asked how long the fly season lasted. Days? Weeks? Maybe we could camp and wait them out. Our spirits sank with his reply: "They're like this all summer long."

We got back on our bikes and "edno, dvei ... damn" they were back. We refitted our bandannas and pedaled on—dreaming of barking dogs, whining children, honking cars, lawn mowers, jet skis, anything ... anything, but the song of the *muxi*.

Razor Burn

LENGTHY, MULTICOUNTRY, MULTILINGUAL JOURNEYS PRESENT A traveler with daily challenges: asking directions; shopping in the market; and inquiring, "Where is the toilet?" They also present occasional challenges such as ordering in a restaurant or sending parcels back home. Before I discovered a failproof method, one task I used to avoid at all costs was getting a haircut.

Let's face it, if you screw up ordering a meal you may pay with heartburn that lasts, at most, a day. But a bad haircut lingers for weeks, months even. The problem lies in the endless interpretations of phrases like "just a trim" and "keep the sideburns."

Throughout my travels, I've discovered that nearly every barber on the planet owns an electric razor. Each comes with a set of guides, numbered 1 to 4, based on how much (or little) hair they leave behind. Number 1 is the shortest (marine recruit length) and number 4 is the longest (still extremely short, but fuzzy objects no longer cling to your head as if it were Velcro).

With this knowledge I can simply hold up four fingers and point to the razor, showing that I want the back and sides buzzed. Then with a gesture I can show I'd like a little trimmed off the top. This allows me to get the same practical, semifashionable haircut in Budapest as I would in Bombay without uttering a single word.

In Blagoevgrad, Bulgaria, twenty kilometers east of the Macedonian border, I decided it was time for my traveler's cut. I overheard someone speaking English at a café and asked her where I might find a good barber. She told me I was in luck, because the best hairstylist in the city worked across the street.

I entered the salon, wary of the prices, and asked how much it would cost to get my hair cut—not shampooed or styled or blown dry—simply cut. I was shocked. When converted to U.S. currency, the price came to less than seventy-five cents. Not only was I about to receive one of the finest haircuts of my life, but one of the cheapest as well.

My stylist, a slender woman in her twenties with short jet black hair, immediately understood my speechless instructions and grabbed for her clippers and popped in the number 4 attachment. With confidence, I leaned back in the chair and paged through the Bulgarian equivalent of *People* magazine. She quickly finished with the razor and went to work trimming with scissors.

Halfway through, I noticed she kept combing my hair forward. I caught her attention and with a gesture showed that I normally combed my hair back, then I returned to an in-depth article about one of Cher's ex-husbands.

She clicked the razor back on. Seconds later a huge tuft of hair fell to the floor. A portion of my scalp felt strangely cool. I looked up into the mirror. A wide swath of stubble, like a bad forest clear-cut, ran directly down the middle of my head. It was too late to protest. The damage had been done.

Something had been lost in the translation. Her interpretation of my gesture was that I had changed my mind and now wanted my whole head shaved. From the aggressive way she proceeded to scrape the razor across my head, she was not pleased with my apparent dissatisfaction with her sense of style. There was nothing I could do but watch the hair fall, trying not to look shocked as large chunks fell into my lap. It wasn't her fault, after all.

My failproof method had failed and I looked in the mirror at a style three-sixteenths of an inch shy of Seattle Mariner's right fielder, Jay Buhner's.

I forced a smile as I paid my bill, gave her a tip ... and reached for my baseball cap.

Highway Robbery

I SAW THE KNIFE. THREE MEN BLOCKED OUR WAY ON A LONELY stretch of highway five miles outside of Kukës, Albania. My initial reaction was not one of fear, but the thought, "I wonder if we'll lose our bikes?"

Without warning, the men brandished clubs. Then they attacked.

Ninety seconds of confusion and horror followed, then stunned silence and tears. Kat and I stood bruised and bloody in the middle of the road, watching the robbers flee up into the scraggy mountain brush with our cameras, passports, and nineteen dollars in cash.

I waved my throbbing arms as best I could at the first vehicle that approached us. I watched the driver's eyes as he made the decision to stop, rather than run us over (we could easily have been decoys for an ambush). The Mercedes skidded to a stop and two well-dressed couples emerged to assist us.

They sat us both down on the side of the highway. Kat's head was bleeding from a nasty gash. One of the women took out a pack of cigarettes.

Kat put up her hand, "No thanks. I don't smoke."

The woman laughed. Then grabbed a half a dozen cigarettes, broke them open, and began applying the tobacco to Kat's wound. The nicotine worked as an astringent to stop the flow of blood.

Villagers from nearby now began arriving and a crowd developed.

We were alive. The worst was over. Or so we thought.

The policeman arrived at the scene of the crime, forty-five minutes later, on a bus. After assessing the situation, he realized he had a problem. He needed to get Kat and me (and our bikes) back to the police station, but he had no vehicle. Easily solved. He simply pointed his gun and stopped the first truck that came our way and accused the driver of being involved in the crime.

This was northern Albania, the Wild West of Europe, where nothing made sense or had a sense of order. The driver had no choice but to become an unwilling civil servant and drive us into town.

Kat and I held on to each other as the truck bumped along the highway and my mind wandered.

Of all the countries in the Balkans, Albania held the most mystery. Centuries of blood vendettas had preceded the reign of Enver Hoxha (1944–1985). His eccentric, paranoid nature left Albania isolated and strewn with over three hundred thousand concrete bunkers, built to ward off certain attack.

When we cycled across the border from Macedonia at Peshkopi, it was as if we had cycled across an era and a continent. We'd struggled along a "main" road fit only for donkeys and four-wheel-drive vehicles. There were no signs, no billboards, no electricity, no kids wearing Chicago Bulls T-shirts (as in the rest of Eastern Europe).

Everything felt foreign, including the language. Albanian (Shqiptimi) is an Indo-European dialect of ancient Illyrian and has no living relative on the planet. I kept commenting to Kat that northern Albania felt more like remote parts of India than anything European.

The road twisted and turned along the gorge of the Drin River. Brown, jagged mountains surrounded us and we gazed up at patches of green farmland that somehow had been carved out of stone.

At one point during a rain shower, we cycled around a bend, only to encounter a funeral procession. More than a hundred men, dressed completely in black, all carrying black umbrellas, slowly marched behind a hand-drawn cart that contained the coffin. This scene, with the stark backdrop of mountains sprinkled with the ever-present concrete bunkers, is etched in my memory.

We had looked forward to difficult but rewarding travels in this, the Land of the Eagle....

The truck lurched to a halt. We had arrived back in Kukës.

At the police station, cigarette smoke filled the drab concrete interrogation room as more and more men squeezed their way in.

The noise level grew as they bickered among themselves trying to get a better look at the Americans.

Kat's head had begun to bleed again, but no one would respond to my pleas to get a cloth or bandage, anything. I finally took off my T-shirt and handed it to her.

More smoke and more noise. I couldn't take it anymore. I stood up and whistled, yelling at them to shut up and go away. It didn't matter what I said. They couldn't understand a word, but now they spoke in muffled tones and several shuffled out of the room.

The chief of police entered, dragging another reluctant civil servant—our interpreter—a local businessman who had the misfortune of being fluent in English. The chief sat across from us and set down a single sheet of white paper someone handed him from the back of the room.

Now we could get down to serious police work. The chief asked us to tell him exactly what happened.

For the next forty-five minutes, through our interpreter, we recalled our story. During this time he wrote exactly three words on the sheet of paper. What were they? Bread, milk, eggs? Who knows.

All the while the typist sat at the other end of the table with his arms folded. The chief asked one final question. "Is anyone in this room involved in the crime?" The poor truck driver cowered in the corner. We quickly cleared his name.

The chief stood up, satisfied with his three-word report, and exited the room, followed by most of the others. Thank God it was over. The typist now inserted a form in triplicate and asked us to tell him exactly what had happened. It started all over again.

In the midst of our second marathon questioning session I leaned over to Kat and asked, "Ninety more seconds with the robbers, or four and a half more hours with the police, which would you choose?"

The wonderful and horrible thing about adventures is that you are not allowed to pick and choose which elements you'll experience. The insanity of the police station and the emotions and images wrapped up in those ninety seconds on the highway were so intense—and still loomed so large—that they threatened to drown out all other memories of our trip like a loud siren that pierces an otherwise peaceful night.

What now?

Did we want to continue our journey in Albania and risk another robbery, or worse?

It would be so easy to get on the first bus or train heading for Athens. We could be on a flight back home and leave it all behind.

We had a decision to make.

Heading for Home

WE WALKED IN THROUGH THE HIGH-WALLED GATE, THROUGH double sets of thick, lead doors and up to the counter at the U.S. Embassy in Tirana, Albania. Having been robbed, we needed new passports. We asked the woman behind the counter where we could get photos taken and where we could use a fax. She had no idea. "What have other Americans done who have been in the same situation?" we asked. "You don't understand. Americans don't travel in Albania, especially in the region you were in. It's too dangerous."

We'd heard this before. The wrongly accused truck driver had driven us back to a nearby village. We limped up to the home of the family who had so kindly housed and fed us the night before. They welcomed us again with open arms. To be among friends, even if we had known them only a few hours, was comforting.

The two eldest sons agreed to drive us to the capitol city of Tirana. There we could get new passports.

The winding, desolate trip in their mini-van complete with horror stories of ambushings and killings took away the disappointment of not being able to cycle the route.

When they dropped us off near the embassy, they made us promise we would not cycle anymore in Albania. It was easy to consent while our bodies still ached. We were scared. But after a couple of days when we arrived at the U.S. Embassy to pick up our new passports, we were reconsidering.

To not get back on the bikes would be to admit defeat—to allow the thieves to steal much more than passports, cameras, and money. Would we allow them to steal our adventurous spirits as well?

We took the train to the coast to avoid the insane drivers of Tirana and got back on our bikes. We pedaled along the coast, gazing out at the blue-green water that led to islands and, somewhere out there, Italy.

That night as we set up our tent on a flat patch of rocky ground, far from the highway, you could feel the tension. Finally Kat broke the silence and said, "Tell me we're going to be okay." For the first time in my travel career, I looked out at desolate mountains and I was afraid. I hated the thieves for that feeling so much more than for the bumps and bruises.

The morning brought clear skies and a little less fear. Our coastal road was not without tensions, however. Little kids threw rocks at us, when they weren't throwing rocks at goats … or each other. People laughed as their dogs chased us and one motorist drove straight at us, only to swerve to avoid us at the last second. He smiled back at us … only joking.

Albania had a rawness to it I've felt nowhere else. It was the best and the worst of our trip concentrated down to a few days. Never had I seen such beauty as in its rugged mountains and coastline. The hospitality of people who took us in rivaled that of any country in Eastern Europe. But with that rawness came a tension, a sense of danger that rarely left us.

By the time we cycled into Sarande and took the ferry to the island of Corfu in Greece we were ready for some well-deserved R & R.

We reflected on our entire trip together. The robbery had tipped the scale toward fear. We began piling up memories to offset its weight: Eating fresh raspberries on the side of the road in Hungary. The scores of women who had adopted Kat in Romania. The field workers in Bulgaria who had scooped pitchforks full of hay to give us a soft place on which to pitch our tent. Acre upon acre of red peppers and the Macedonian family who filled us with the divine spread made from them called *ajvar* (eye-vaar). The lonely stretch of Albania along the river on which we felt more like explorers than travelers.

Each country brought a different flood of memories, meals, conversations, and relationships. And each helped put the terror we had experienced into perspective.

A couple of weeks and a few beaches and islands later, we walked through the gates of the Acropolis in Athens. "What is the date?" Kat asked as we gazed up at the columns of the Parthenon. It was September 30—only three days later than we had planned to meet, back when I was on a solo journey.

We were finally able to look at each other and ask the question: If we had the choice to live this trip over again, including the robbery, would we? The answer was a resounding "yes."

We had been through so much together: sickness, storms, fatigue, and fear. Thousands of kilometers of winding, dusty roads that led to villages, vistas, and people we will never forget.

But now it was time to find a travel agent and a cheap airline ticket, buy a few souvenirs, box the bikes, and head for home.

Our trip was over, but our adventure will continue ... for soon after we return to Seattle, surrounded by family and friends, my travel companion will become my wife.

Acknowledgments

SOLO ADVENTURES ARE RARELY SOLO.

I would like to thank Brian Higham and the entire staff at public radio station KUOW who first aired my aerograms sent from India; Jim Molnar of *The Seattle Times* who acknowledged the writer in me; Allen Noren, who originally edited the South Africa pieces, for a constant flow of advice and encouragement; and Joe Kurmaskie who helped bring the fun back.

And to Kat Marriner—friend, travel companion, and wife— life and this book would not be complete without you.